Every Child an Artist! New Methods and Materials for Elementary Art

Barbara Ann Beswick

photographs by *James F. Beswick, Jr.*

Barbara Beswick has taught art in the Chester, New Jersey, school system for over 15 years. She is a graduate of Kutztown State College and has studied at The American University, Washington, D.C., Tyler School of Temple University, Trenton State College, and Jersey City State College, as well as in South America and Europe.

Named one of the country's top ten art teachers by *Teacher Magazine*, Barbara Beswick was nominated for "National Teacher of the Year," and is listed in "Outstanding Elementary Teachers of America." Many of her articles have appeared in *School Arts Magazine* and *Teacher Magazine*.

Mrs. Beswick resides in Salt Lake City, Utah, with her husband and young son.

Parker Publishing Company, Inc.
West Nyack, New York

© 1983, by

PARKER PUBLISHING COMPANY, INC.

West Nyack, N. Y.

All rights reserved. No part of this book may be reproduced in any form or by any means, without permission in writing from the publisher.

Library of Congress Cataloging in Publication Data

Beswick, Barbara Ann
   Every child an artist!

   Includes index.
   1. Art—Study and teaching (Elementary)   2. Activity programs in education.   I. Beswick, James F.   II. Title.
N350.B43   1983   372.5'044   82-24626
ISBN 0-13-293324-1

Printed in the United States of America

This book is due, in large part, to the support and guidance of my husband, Jim. Without his confidence in me, it would still be an idea, floating about, looking for a place to settle. Therefore, I dedicate the book to him.

About these arts and crafts lessons

Teaching art for many years to elementary- through high-school-aged children has been a privilege and a joy. The enthusiasm generated in the students by an unusual but classic approach to teaching has, in return, been a stimulus for my own constant flow of ideas. The lessons in this book are my "inventions," using unusual ways to teach basic concepts of art and the principles by which all art can be approached by each student.

This collection of arts and crafts lessons is for the classroom teacher as well as the art instructor. Emphasis is placed on the students' learning particular skills, techniques, and use of media, while enjoying the creation of a finished product. All lessons are presented with simple, step-by-step directions. You need not have any particular talent in art to effectively teach these lessons and see results.

All projects are designated for specific grade levels, and most lessons cover several levels. But this should not confine you in any way. If a class is composed of a group of more highly skilled students whose abilities and enthusiasm run above the average, consider lessons that are specified for a higher level. Naturally, the opposite plan should be considered if the group is below average in performance. Once instructions are given, students can proceed at their own level with acceptable results for all, regardless of ability or talent.

Since most of the lessons cross over two or more grade levels, they can be used for an art curriculum guide to cover an entire school year. Time set aside for art may be occasional or on a regular basis of once a week or twice a month, and the time slot anywhere from one-half hour to an hour. Uses, notes, and variations are included with the lessons to enhance a particular subject or holiday.

My philosophy of teaching art, evolved through years of working with students, teachers, and parents, is that children's capabilities can exceed the expectations we often hold for them. I assume that *all* children are capable of doing more complicated tasks and comprehending more detailed information than we *think* they can—and I insist on it! The lessons developed for my students are based on techniques and ideas that are a little more mature and advanced than expected for the particular age suggested, but the built-in flexibility of each lesson assures one hundred percent success.

Although the final outcome should not be emphasized as the most important part of an art endeavor, the results that students get from their involvement should provide a sense of accomplishment and satisfaction in their performance along with the appreciation and knowledge gained in the process.

I hope using these unusual lessons will bring you the same happiness and pride of achievement I have seen in my classes. If the teacher enjoys the task, the students certainly will.

Barbara Ann Beswick

Tips on tools and supplies

The following presents suggestions for obtaining and using the art materials needed for the lessons in this book. Included are ideas for getting free materials, substituting less expensive supply items where possible, and providing appropriate tools for younger and older children. There are also hints for sharing, storing, and maintaining materials that will save you time, money and work.

"Throw-away" Items

At the beginning of the school year, send a note home to parents asking them to save any "throw-away" items that may be put to use in the arts and crafts lessons. "Just look around your basement or attic and keep us in mind when you are cleaning out closets!"

The items you might ask for are:

magazines
newspapers
cardboard scraps
wood scraps
cloth scraps
felt scraps
wallpaper samples
yarn and string scraps
tin cans (washed and labels removed)
juice concentrate cans
coffee cans
plastic containers with lids
wire coat hangers
color-coded telephone wire (usually in bundles or wrapped in a plastic covering)

polyethylene sheeting scraps (used in new house construction as a vapor barrier)
foam padding (from wall-to-wall carpeting installation or upholstering)
oil base and enamel paints
legs cut from jeans
sponges
cotton swabs
smocks or shirts
socks
pantyhose
gloves and mittens
costume jewelry, sequins, beads, buttons
artificial flowers and plants
florist's clay
butter knives and spoons
shells, driftwood, seeds, pods, beans, feathers, nuts, etc.
wigs and hairpieces

Supply Items

All of the following items can be ordered through most supply houses. You may find it more economical and/or convenient to order them on a shared basis with other teachers rather than individually.

Paper

Construction Paper: 9" x 12", 12" x 18", and 18" x 24" sheets of construction paper in assorted colors are needed.

Drawing Paper: 9" x 12", 12" x 18", 18" x 24", and 24" x 36" white vellum drawing paper is needed.

Manila or Mimeo Scraps: 9" x 12" manila or mimeo scraps used for planning or practice sketching are usually available from your school's office.

Oaktag or Cardboard: Oaktag is rather expensive but rolls smoothly; in most cases it may be substituted with semi-smooth, gray cardboard. When oaktag is called for as a base to be covered, use cut-up cardboard boxes instead.

Scrap Box: Keep a box handy for scrap colored paper. Faded or torn bulletin board background paper can be saved, along with "mistake" papers of students. Every so often, dump all but the largest pieces and start again.

Wallpaper: Go through wallpaper samples discriminately and eliminate any picture samples or inappropriate designs. Most samples can effectively be used for design work and craft projects.

Newspaper: Keep a supply of newspaper to cover desks, tables, or floor when doing messy projects. Be aware that some markers "bleed" through some papers, so back the work with newspaper or scrap paper.

Magazines: Start a collection from your school library's throwaways. *National Geographic, Ranger Rick, Zoo News,* and *Audubon* are good samples. Weekly news magazines provide famous faces and cartoon ideas that are needed for some of the lessons.

Newsprint Paper: An inexpensive grade of paper, it can be used for preliminary sketching and for printing. 12" x 18" is the best size because it can be cut down if smaller sizes are needed.

Cutting Tools

Scissors: Regular school scissors are appropriate for the lessons. Blunt-tipped types are better for young students; pointed scissors are fine for grade levels 2-6.

Dressmaker's Scissors: When material has to be cut, provide several pairs of large dressmaker's scissors. Do not use these for paper or cardboard.

Manicure Scissors: These come in handy for some fine cutting work. Keep a pair handy. Older students might be asked to bring these, in a safe manner.

Razors and Knives: Try to avoid the use of knives and razors with the students. Do anything of this nature yourself.

Paper Cutter: It saves a lot of time and work and helps with mounting or matting art work. Some lessons call for specific paper sizes. By the nature of the instructions, you will know whether or not accuracy is important. If students need half of a standard 9" x 12" construction paper, give the paper out to be folded, cut, and shared. If accuracy is essential and you cannot cut for your students for lack of a paper cutter, have two or three students work on paper preparation for you ... measuring and/or folding a few sheets at a time and cutting with good scissors. Cutting more than three peices of paper at once will ruin accuracy as the papers tend to slide apart while you are cutting.

Drawing Tools

Pencils: 2B lead pencils are easily erased and write darker than harder lead pencils.

Tips on tools and supplies

Marking Pens: These are suggested for many lessons, with crayons as an alternative. Although expensive, a few sets of non-toxic markers can prove themselves in the quality of the drawing you will get from the students; just do not let them "color in" with the markers, as that will dry them of color in a flash! How can the students fill in with markers to get a special background effect? Look at Figures A-1, A-2, and A-3.

Crayons: These can be arranged by colors in tin cans, with each can covered with the corresponding colored paper. This arrangement allows you to have colors available for special work that requires each student to have the same color crayon. (Have you ever tried to find a black crayon in a hurry and all you can find is purple?) It also helps you to reorder particular colors when they run out. Line up the cans for easy access in the middle of the work area when doing crayon projects; stack the cans pyramid-style when not in use. Once a year, replace the paper to keep the colors bright.

Oil Crayons: These are suggested for one of the lessons and are expensive. A few boxes can equip a class, and the oil-painting-like quality they lend is very effective.

Chalks or Pastels: Any type of colored chalks will do as long as they are "soft." Hard chalks do not work very well on construction paper, although they do work fine with white drawing paper. Most "board chalks" are soft and will suffice.

Charcoal: Either sticks or pencils (which are more expensive) are fine for the charcoal lessons.

Colored Pencils: These are suggested for some lessons because of their delicacy. A few sets will be adequate for the whole class, but do not allow sharpening on a regular pencil sharpener; if hand sharpeners are used, the pencils will last longer. Extremely sharp points are not necessary, so less sharpening between uses will also make the pencils last longer.

Glue and Paste

Glue: Use regular white glue for most projects with older students. It holds better than paste although it takes a bit more time to dry. To apply to small bits of paper or to tiny areas, use toothpicks, popsicle sticks, or cotton swabs. Brushes can also be used to apply glue, but be sure to wash them in warm, soapy water immediately after the lesson. For large areas, let the students use their fingers to apply glue. Keep the glue in five or more margarine tubs because it is more economical to buy white glue by the gallon and put it in separate containers. With the lids snapped in place, the glue does not harden. Keep damp rags handy so that the students can wipe excess glue off their hands intermittently throughout the lesson.

Paste: It can be used for younger students' paper projects. A dollop of paste on a bit of scrap paper is enough for two or three students to share.

Tips on tools and supplies 13

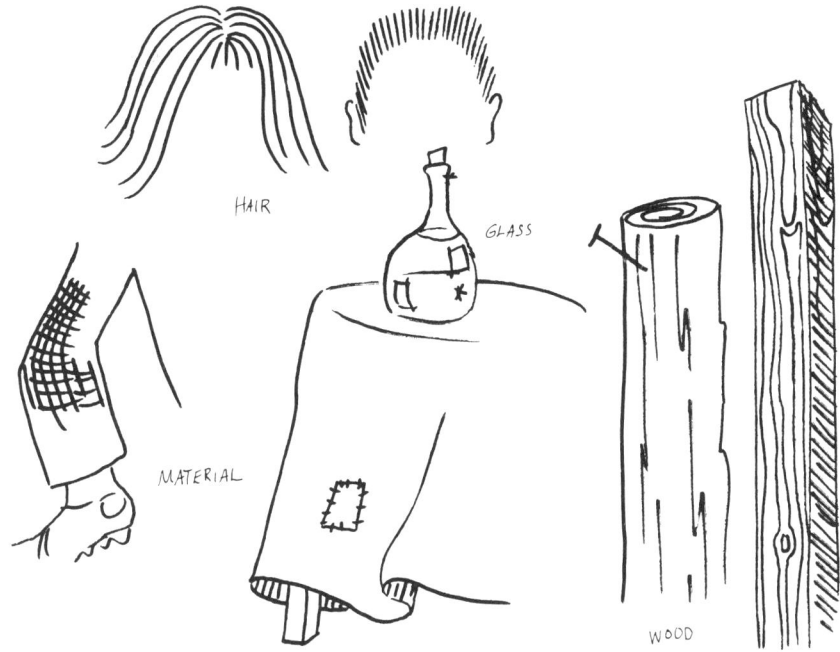

Figure A-1

Figure A-2

14   *Tips on tools and supplies*

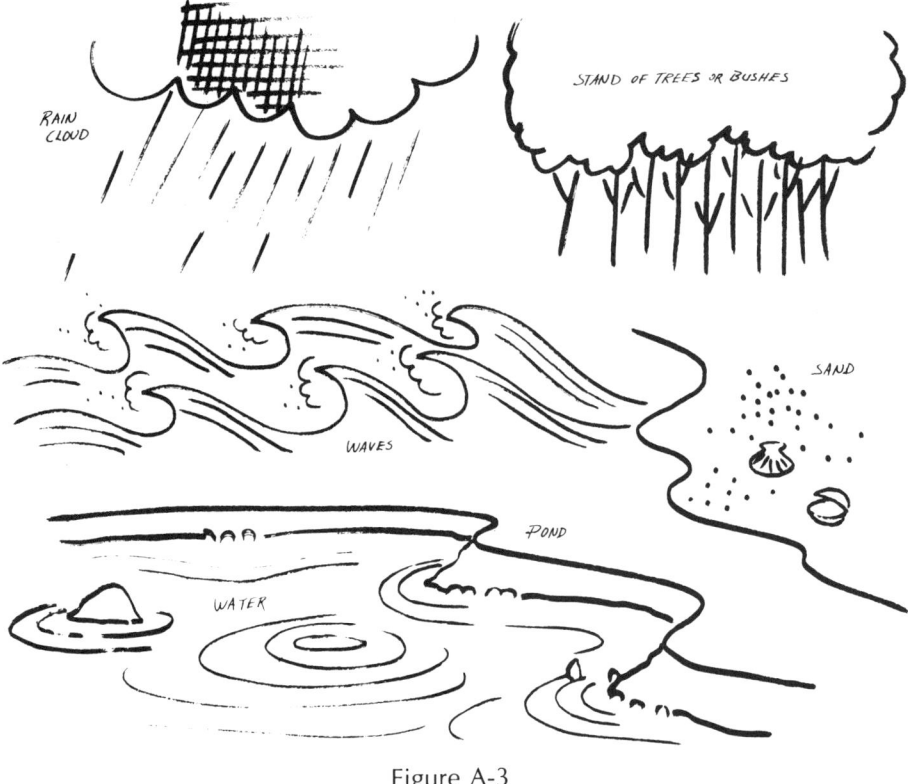

Figure A-3

Do not forget to scrape the unused paste back into the jar and to keep the lid on tight; paste dries out very fast. Water can be added if it gets too dry, but not if it gets to the crumbly stage.

Painting Supplies

Watercolors: A few boxes of watercolors can be shared by the whole class. Order the kind that can be refilled.

Poster Paints: These are less expensive by the quart and will keep nicely if you do not allow students to paint directly from the jars. Use a spoon and dip out some thick paint into a plastic container or coffee can. Add water and stir to a creamy consistency. Unused paint can be saved by covering the container with a snap-on lid. The paint jar should be tightly closed and even taped shut if it is to be stored for a long period of time.

Bleach: Household bleach is needed for one lesson. Use your common sense and do not keep the bottle open for a long period of time.

Brushes: An array of brushes are handy, but a few of each kind will do. A dozen or so each of small, medium, and large brushes will cover just about any need. Be sure to thoroughly clean them after each use with warm, soapy water, dry them by squeezing the hairs out gently between your fingers, and allow them to dry lying flat. After they are dry, store them with hairs up, in a can. Dirty water left under the ferrule (the metal strip that holds the hairs in) will eventually rot the brush, so do not stand them upright until they are dry.

Sponges: Some painting lessons require sponges, so keep a supply of small pieces and larger whole sponges handy.

Brayers: These are rolling applicators for ink or paint used in printing. You might be able to borrow them from a junior high or high school art department.

Miscellaneous Items

Rulers: Rulers are called for in some lessons, but more than likely *not* for measuring, so any straightedge will do. If you prefer, cut oaktag or cardboard into 2" x 12" strips and use for making straight lines.

Compasses: These are needed to draw circles, but again, anything round will do in most cases. Assorted tin cans, rolls of tape, small buttons, and coins provide a variety of circle sizes. For one lesson, compasses are used to punch holes. Perhaps nails or large needles will do instead.

Tape: Masking tape is needed for many lessons, but not in excess. Width is important—the wider the tape, the better it will hold, especially if you need to hang things or mount them on another paper. Order one-inch tape for most of your work and two-inch tape for mounting and display work.

Stapler: Required for some lessons, it is for your use only. Sometimes a small stapler is easier to use, as in the case of Origami Hand Puppets in Chapter 2.

Research/Audio-Visual: Some of the lessons require a research book or two, and, in one lesson, a film. Hopefully, you have access to a school or community library to locate these rather common items. Some of the materials may already be in your possession in your private book collection or on the shelf in your classroom.

Tips on tools and supplies

CONTRIBUTING ARTISTS

My thanks to all of the following children for permitting me to photograph their art work as examples of the lessons in this book.

Katie Ananson	Gina Lucas
Loren Austin	George Luzniak
Joe Barberi	Greg Luzniak
Cindy Barker	Craig McDonald
Kristin Bauer	Bryan McGurn
Kurt Beswick	Chrissy Mitchell
Lisa Boehs	Susan Nelson
Chris Cox	Mike Nervine
Peter Drysdale	Lisa Norby
Nicole Eller	Kristin Plank
Rusty Fagan	Brett Raimondo
Matthew Fremont	Susan Runk
Laura Gahtan	Scott Scanlan
Kristin Gorman	Lisa Schuetz
Jeff Grimm	Jay Stark
Gregg Groff	Julie Steinfield
Jeff Hauck	Denny Strange
Robbie Helgans	Christopher Tanis
Brian Hoffman	Amy Tiedemann
Jim Hoffman	Richard von Woerkom
Jesse Kagan	Kerri Westover
Victoria Kohlmaier	April Whorley
Mike Krause	Susan Willenborg
Kevin Lovejoy	Kevin Wright

Table of Contents

About These Arts and Crafts Lessons 7
Tips on Tools and Supplies 9
Contributing Artists 16

1. Have Fun with Paper and Learn a Few New Tricks 21

    SSSSnakes! (snake design mobile) K-3 • 22
    Tearing into Spring (torn-paper animals) K-3 • 25
    Which Came First? (pop-art cartoons) 2-5 • 29
    Yakkety-Yak (paper mouth puppet) 3-5 • 32
    No-Mess Mobile (paper sculpture) 4-5 • 34
    Aren't Those B—B—Bones? (skeleton study) 5-6 • 37

2. Paper Turns into Many Items with a Little Help from Your Friends . . . 41

    Light Snow Falling (perforated light pictures of snowmen) 3-5 • 42
    Look, Mom, Hands! (cut paper Easter rabbit) 4-5 • 45
    Animals Can Talk, Too (Origami hand puppet) 3-6 • 49
    You'll Love These (valentine cards) 4-6 • 56
    Let's Pitch a Tent (paper models for outdoor scenes) 4-6 • 60
    Making a Scene (three-dimensional scenery) 5-6 • 65
    Look Out! I Can See You (characters with roving eyes) 5-6 • 69
    That's Strange (distortion of a magazine picture) 5-6 • 74
    Photo Potpourri (picture humor and mystery) 5-6 • 78
    The Paper Connection Caper (figures from a basic pattern) 6 • 81
    Say It with Letters (block letters) 6 • 85

3. Print and Repeat for Good Times and Good Things 90

    Pussy Willows in a Pot (fingerprints) K-3 • 91
    Symmetrical Scaries (easy Halloween drawing and printing) 3-6 • 94

18   **Contents**

And NOW...in the Center Ring (charcoal circus printing) 3-6 • **98**
Please Repeat Yourself (bas-relief crayon rubbings) 4-6 • **101**
Didn't I Just See That? (carbon paper designs) 5-6 • **104**
Stamp, Stamp, Stamp (clay presses) 5-6 • **107**

4. Draw Out Your Students' Talents **112**

Grow Potted Plants (simple plant drawing) K-2 • **113**
Scribble Scrabble (a drawing game or test) K-6 • **116**
If You Laugh, I'll Cry (facial expressions) 3-5 • **119**
Scissors Sillies (trace-around cartoons) 3-6 • **123**
It Won't Rub Off on Me (polyethylene sheeting and crayons) 3-6 • **125**
Getting into Things (perspective) 3-5 • **128**
Trees with U's and V's (drawing trees) 4-6 • **135**
Hearts and Flowers (Pennsylvania Dutch art) 4-6 • **140**

5. Everyone's an Artist! **144**

Starting with Something (elaborating upon a line drawing) 4-6 • **145**
Rough and Tumble (winter action figures) 4-6 • **148**
That's My Name—Want My Address? (letter and name designs) 4-6 • **152**
Using Your Thumb (symmetrical object drawing) 5-6 • **155**
I Gotta Hand It to Ya (contour drawing cartoons) 5-6 • **159**
Mug Shots (profiles and frontals) 6 • **163**
You Take One Half, I'll Take the Other (complete a face) 6 • **167**
Buildings in Depth (two-point perspective) 6 • **170**

6. Crafts Made with Unusual Materials **179**

Don't Shake My Hand...It Bites! (puppet on a hand) K-2 • **180**
Cute Cutoffs (shirt sleeves as puppet clothes) K-3 • **183**
Let Your Fingers Do the Talking (cloth and magazine finger puppet) K-6 • **186**
Hooray! I've Lost a Mitten (mitten and glove characters) 2-6 • **189**
It's Raining Cats and Dogs (clay bead jewelry) 4-6 • **192**
Hello! We're Weaving (telephone wire mobile) 5-6 • **196**
Three-Dimensional Poetry (sculptures and creative writing) 5-6 • **201**
Heigh-Ho, the Dairy-O, the Farmer Is a Doll (stuffed doll) 5-6 • **205**
More and More Books (marbleized paper notebooks) 5-6 • **209**
Who's That? (foam masks and head gear) 6 • **215**
I'm Almost as Big as You Are! (stocking marionettes) 6 • **218**

7. New Dimensions in Painting **234**

   Hey, That's Me! (body tracing) K-1 • **235**
   Big Green Dragon (brayer painting) K-3 • **238**
   Stone Age Cave Paintings (chalk drawings) 4-6 • **241**
   Bleaching Everything But the Laundry (designs on material and paper) 4-6 • **245**
   Blow-Up Cartoons (graphing from small to large) 5-6 • **248**

Index **253**

1
Have fun with paper and learn a few new tricks

Paper crafts for children need to be simple so as not to cause frustration, but exciting enough to turn them on. These are! The lessons are easy to do, yet each one teaches the children a new method or skill that can be transferred to more advanced techniques in later craft experiences.

———————— ssssnakes ————————
(snake design mobile)

Grade Levels: K-3   **Time Needed: 40 minutes**

Before You Begin:

Display several pictures of snakes and discuss the varieties, sizes, colors, and other details, gearing your discussion to the interest and age of your students. Show the students how to make one of the snakes described here so that they can see how easily they can draw a spiral. It might be a good idea to have two or three other snakes already drawn to demonstrate the many ways the snakes can be decorated, using various design elements.

Objectives:

- To introduce students to basic design elements (line, shape, color, pattern) and vocabulary (design, pattern, spiral).
- To provide new techniques with crayons.
- To practice consistency in drawing and coloring.
- To provide experience in cutting and in making something three dimensional from a two-dimensional surface.
- To learn about snakes through observation.

Materials:

- crayons
- 9" x 12" oaktag
- scissors
- string
- hole puncher

Procedure:

1. With a crayon, draw a small circle in the center of the oaktag.
2. Starting at the circle, draw a spiral, taking care not to cross over

any lines. Make the spiral at least one-half to two inches wide as the crayon moves away from the circle.

3. End the spiral by connecting the "head" of the snake to its "body." (See Figure 1-1.)

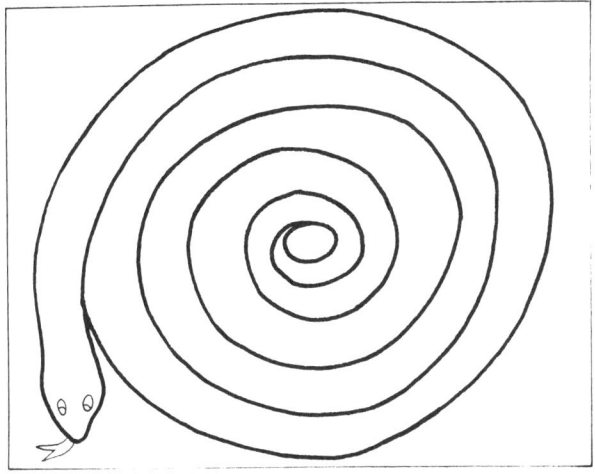

Figure 1-1

4. Add a tongue and eyes to complete the snake.

5. Decorate the snake by repeating a pattern from the head around to the tail. (See Figure 1-2.) Show the students the many shapes and lines they can use to develop a repeat pattern. Color the design in but encourage thorough coloring or the snake will be drab.

6. Turn the oaktag over and decorate this side. Hold two or more crayons together and make stripes, plaids, or swirls. Or, make polka dots, X's, or zigzags. Be sure to color areas in solidly.

7. Turn the oaktag back to the snake side and cut along the outside line of the snake shape. Then cut into and along the spiral, starting where the head touches the body.

8. Discard the center circle. Punch a hole through either the head or the tail and pull a piece of string through.

9. Hang the snake mobile from the ceiling, a window, or chalkboard, or students may want their "pet" on their shoulders!

NOTE: Although this activity might be done with colored construction paper, the finished snake will not be as sturdy as when made with oaktag.

24 **Have fun with paper**

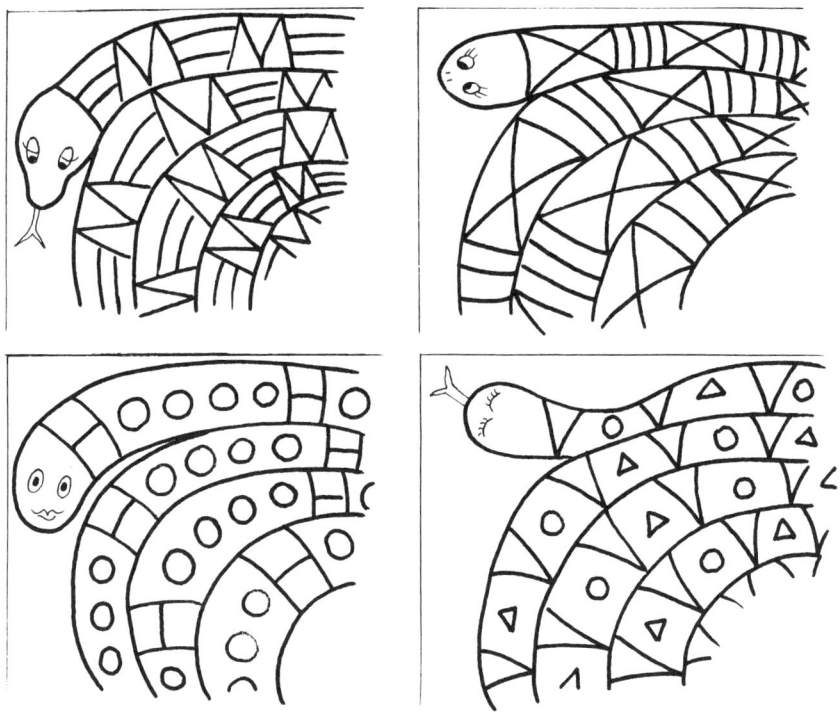

Figure 1-2

tearing into spring
(torn-paper animals)

Grade Levels: K-3   **Time Needed: 40 minutes**

Before You Begin:

Spring and Easter sprout thoughts of fluffy bunnies, chicks, ducklings, and bears. Bring these animals to life by showing a few examples of torn-paper animals in various scenes. (See Figures 1-3, 1-4, 1-5, and 1-6.) Explain that the paper tearing is easy to do and that the look of fur or down will result from this tearing rather than from cutting.

Objectives:

- To develop small motor coordination and manipulative skills.
- To provide a simple means of expression that does not result in discouragement.
- To encourage planning and "thinking ahead."

Materials:

- 12" x 18" construction paper (assorted colors)
- 4½" x 6" white construction paper
- 4½" x 3" yellow construction paper
- 4½" x 6" brown construction paper
- glue
- crayons or markers
- assorted scrap paper
- scissors

Procedure:

The most important part of this lesson is keeping the fingers of both hands very close together as tearing progresses. Students must look at the whole paper first, and try to visualize the final shape coming from the whole. The entire paper should be used to make one animal shape.

For Chicks

1. Use the 12" x 18" construction paper for the background.
2. Tear the yellow construction paper to form a round shape.
3. Glue the chick to the background paper and add a beak, eyes, and feet with crayons or markers. Add details with crayons, markers, and cut paper.

For Ducklings

1. Use the same basic chick shape, but this time include a neck.
2. Add webbed feet and a larger rounded beak. (See Figure 1-3.)

Figure 1-3

For Rabbits

1. Use the 12" x 18" construction paper for the background.
2. Tear the white construction paper to form a round "puff." Try to tear the ears, tail, and feet along with the main body. If students have difficulty, let them tear the parts separately and glue them to the body.
3. Glue the rabbit to the background paper and add the face, whiskers, pads on paws, and ear interiors. (See Figure 1-4.)

Have fun with paper 27

Figure 1-4

For Bears

1. Save this step for older students as the shapes are more complex.
2. Tear the bear shapes to show bears down on all four feet, or standing on hind legs. Parts of unsuccessful bears can be emerging from caves or hiding behind trees!
3. Add eyes, noses, whiskers, mouths, and claws. (See Figures 1-5 and 1-6.)

Figure 1-5

28   *Have fun with paper*

Figure 1-6

Uses:

These animals may be used in connection with particular holidays. The chicks, ducklings, and rabbits can be used for Easter pictures with baskets and eggs. The bears might illustrate Christmas stories and winter scenes, or maybe a Teddy Bears' Picnic!

Variation:

Other furry animals, such as kittens, squirrels, and shaggy dogs, might be attempted. Any object that is fluffy or furry, such as a cloud or tree leaves, might also be torn. Smooth objects, such as boats, cars, and houses, would not make good subjects for this lesson.

Have fun with paper 29

which came first
(pop-art cartoons)

Grade Levels: 2-5   **Time Needed: 40 minutes**

Before You Begin:

Students are to think of eggs for this activity. What if some of them do not like eggs? That's okay, because they are to think of something funny to do with an egg. How about a fried egg resting on top of a bald head? An egg shell cracked open to reveal a chicken in a nest? Decorated eggs nestled in a basket, but one of them cracked and holding a baby dinosaur?

Show simple cutouts of the different kinds of eggs that can be used for the lesson and then let the students work large and go wild with the paper. (See Figure 1-7.) Encourage the students to make the egg the central object in the picture. Think of titles for the pictures, too. How about "Eggs in Space"? "Funny-Side Up"? "My Pet Egg"? "Egg-Head"?

Figure 1-7

30   *Have fun with paper*

Objectives:

- To encourage creative thinking by using a common object.
- To develop good composition and arrangement techniques.
- To provide an opportunity for comic expression.

Materials:

- 12" x 18" construction paper (assorted colors)
- 6" x 9" white construction paper
- scrap paper
- glue
- scissors
- crayons or markers

Procedure:

1. Make a plan for an egg cutout. Discuss top view, side view.
2. Cut out the egg(s) or egg parts and other background items and arrange on 12" by 18" construction paper. A whole egg may be made easily by folding paper in half and sketching and cutting one half of the egg.

Figure 1-8

3. Do not glue anything in place until all pieces have been cut out so that the composition can be developed. Some overlapping should occur.

4. Cut strips of scrap paper roughly one inch wide and two to three inches long. Roll them into rings and glue to the backs of eggs and other items cut from scrap paper.

5. Draw any details with crayons or markers (see Figure 1-8), but encourage using cut paper for most items. Then arrange and glue the "pop-out" items on the background.

Uses:

These egg ideas could be used to encourage poetry or creative writing. They might also be used for health and nutrition lessons, or to decorate the classroom at Easter.

32 *Have fun with paper*

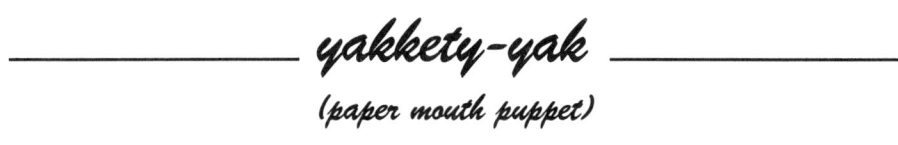

yakkety-yak
(paper mouth puppet)

Grade Levels: 3-5 **Time Needed: 40 to 80 minutes**

Before You Begin:

Make one of these puppets in front of the students and let them watch it emerge. The simplicity of the construction and its amusing character will delight them and stimulate them to create their own puppets. Why not pull out one or two more completed puppets and let them "yak" at each other? Two characters might discuss the day: "Hey, man, what's happening?" "I really like your jacket...." The students will love it, and may want to make two so that they can carry on conversations, too.

Objectives:

- To increase awareness in three-dimensional form.
- To develop manipulative skills through paper sculpture.
- To provide an outlet for physical and verbal expressions.

Materials:

- 9" x 12" construction paper, assorted colors, with plenty of "flesh" colors available
- scissors
- glue
- scraps of paper, yarn, ribbon, material, etc.

Procedure:

1. Fold a sheet of construction paper in half lengthwise so that it is 4½ inches wide.
2. Fold it in half from the bottom. To form a "pocket" for the mouth at the middle fold, fold back both ends of the paper. (See Figure 1-9.)
3. Use the scraps to add ears, a nose, and eyes. A nose can be a rolled cylinder or cone. Cut lips from red paper, and glue along the straight edge of the mouth. Use white paper for teeth and pink paper for a tongue.

Have fun with paper 33

Figure 1-9

4. Make hair by cutting and gluing paper curls, spirals, or strips. Yarn can also be used.

5. Continue by adding freckles, collars, ties, cigars, glasses, necklaces and earrings with cut paper or found items. (See Figure 1-10.) The mouth puppet is now ready to "yakkety-yak."

Figure 1-10

Use:

The puppets might depict specific book or story characters, or particular historical personalities. They might also be the students' self-images who will give reports or autobiographies.

no-mess mobile
(paper sculpture)

Grade Levels: 4-5   **Time Needed: 40 minutes**

Before You Begin:

Discuss with your students the difference between two dimensional and three dimensional. "A piece of paper is flat or two dimensional. How can we make it three dimensional?" Students may suggest folding, rolling, or fan-folding. Demonstrate these methods along with cutting into the paper and twisting the parts away from each other, rolling a cone, folding a square tube, and cutting a spiral. By now, the students should be thinking of other ways to elaborate on these simple sculptural techniques.

Explain to the students that they are going to create no-mess mobiles by using two sandwiched sheets of paper and discovering many different ways to give the paper a third dimension. Anything that is cut cannot be cut off, but must remain attached to the paper and be rolled, folded, or slot-tabbed back to the main body of paper. Thus, a spiral can be cut and then fan-folded to get a circular staircase effect; doors can be cut through the paper that open up to reveal empty space or an interesting design; tabs and slots can help hold it all together. (See Figure 1-11.) Make some examples of these sculpture techniques.

Figure 1-11

Have fun with paper   35

Display several lines that make interesting sculptural shapes after they are separated, twisted, and connected back to the paper with tabs and slots or a stapler. (See Figure 1-12.)

Figure 1-12

Objectives:

- To demonstrate how a two-dimensional surface can become three dimensional.
- To give an opportunity to compose and utilize space to fit students' needs.
- To learn various paper sculptural and connective techniques.
- To practice control with scissors.

Materials:

- 12" x 12" construction paper (assorted colors)
- scissors
- stapler
- string or yarn

Procedure:

1. Choose two sheets of different colored paper
2. Keep the sheets together as one, or separate diagonally and staple at one or two corners.

3. Try as many things as possible with the paper in cutting, folding, rolling, and connecting, but without separating anything from the paper and without using glue.

4. Start by cutting in from corners or edges, or by poking into the paper somewhere in the middle.

5. As the mobile takes shape, see what can be done to give it more dimension. Cut through in a door-like manner to expose the other color; fringe along the edges; crinkle or curl some strips, separating the two colors for more contrast. Staple wherever tabs and slots will not work.

6. Decide how the sculpture should hang and attach yarn or string at the top.

7. Display the mobile in the classroom. For a very nice shadow effect, hang the mobile where light can take advantage of its nooks and crannies. (See Figure 1-13.)

Figure 1-13

Use:

The color choices might be tied in with the season (different shades of green for spring), or a holiday (red and green for Christmas). Remember that no two mobiles will be the same.

Have fun with paper   **37**

_____ *aren't those b — b — bones?* _____
(skeleton study)

Grade Levels: 5-6   **Time Needed: 80-120 minutes**

Before You Begin:

Halloween may be motivation enough for your students to get into skeletons, but the study of bone structure in academic sciences can be just as stimulating. Show an example of a finished skeleton, complete with extra details for a spooky flavor if you are emphasizing Halloween.

Objectives:

- To study and understand human bone structure.
- To develop listening and following-direction skills.
- To present an enjoyable, informal atmosphere for serious study and individual expression.

Materials:

- 9" x 12" white construction paper, or an inexpensive substitute
- 18" x 24" black or dark-colored construction paper
- scissors
- pencils
- newspaper
- glue
- cotton swabs
- scrap paper
- encyclopedias, medical pamphlets, etc., showing skeletal structure
- manicure scissors (optional)

Procedure:

1. Fold or cut eight sheets of white construction paper.
    a. Fold five in half lengthwise.
    b. Fold two in half, end to end.

38   *Have fun with paper*

c. Fold one in half, end to end, and cut along the fold. Fold one of these pieces again, end to end. Use the other piece to draw the skull.

2. Draw the bones on the appropriate pieces of white paper, taking care to draw each bone as large as the paper. Tell students to look at the empty areas in the bones and try to reproduce those shapes as well as the actual bone shapes. This will aid their drawing. Discuss the proper names of the bones. (See Figure 1-14.)

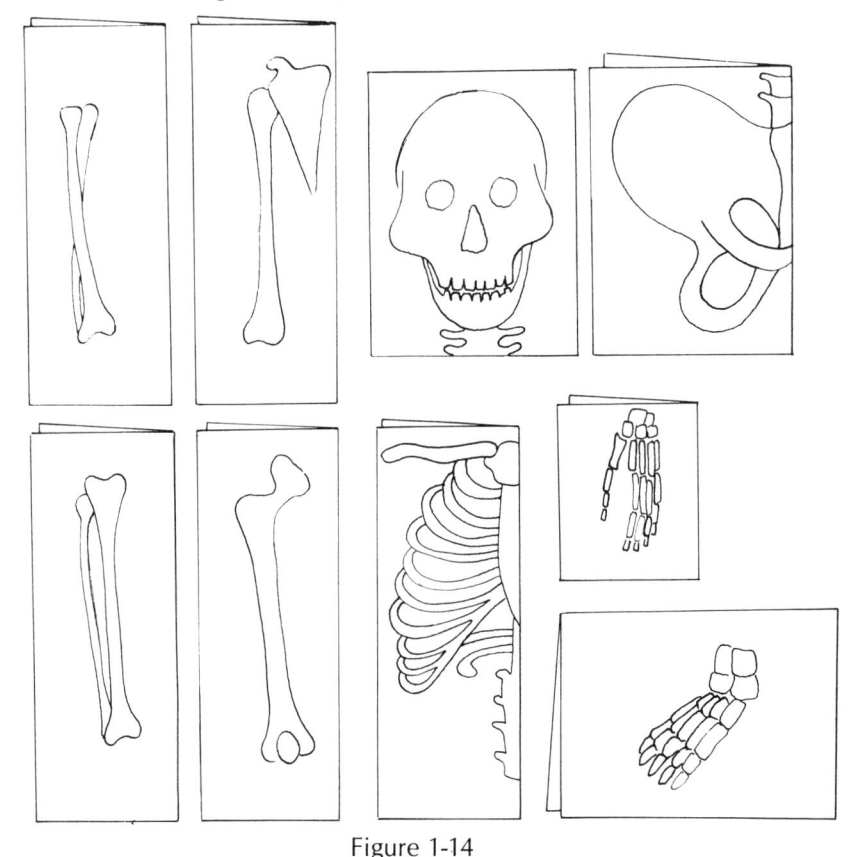

Figure 1-14

3. Begin with the skull and draw a shape that fills the paper. Use scissors to cut out the eye sockets and nasal passages.

4. Draw the bones and remove sections between the lower arm and leg bones, pelvic bone and ribs by poking into the center of sections with scissors points and cutting along the lines. Manicure scissors may be useful here.

Have fun with paper 39

5. Pencil is used to finish details and possibly shade some of the bones. Bones that were cut from double paper should match in appearance.

6. Arrange sheets of dark construction paper on a wall, bulletin board, or chalkboard for the background. Lay out the paper according to the position of each skeleton. Three sheets put together sideways, for example, allow for bending knees and elbows, while two sheets put together lengthwise are fine for a standing skeleton.

7. Glue each bone in place with cotton swabs, using scrap paper to protect the background. Follow a prearranged plan and take care to overlap the bones where necessary, such as at the knees, elbows, and pelvis.

8. Create a different effect by gluing the bones slightly apart from each other to show each bone totally, or introduce a humorous element by mixing up the bones and having the skeleton hold its head in its hand! Make sure students experiment with arrangement before gluing.

9. Use colored scrap paper to decorate the skeleton with a pirate's bandana and eye patch, or a pumpkin in place of a skull, or a ball and chain. (See Figures 1-15 and 1-16.) Be creative. The "rickety rattling" display will certainly stir interest and raise goose bumps, whether for a Halloween celebration or for an academic study of the human body.

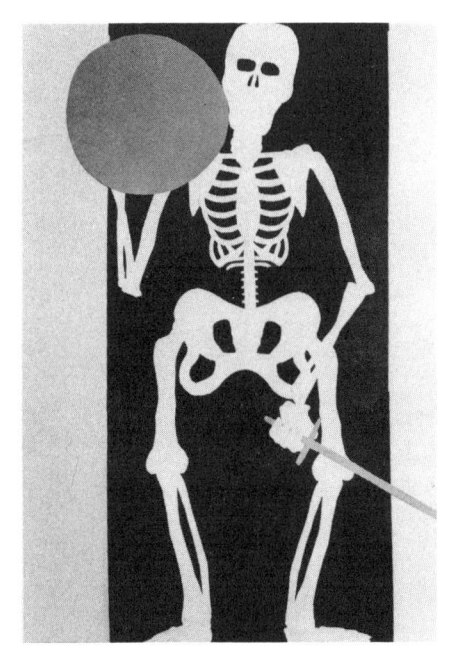

Figure 1-15

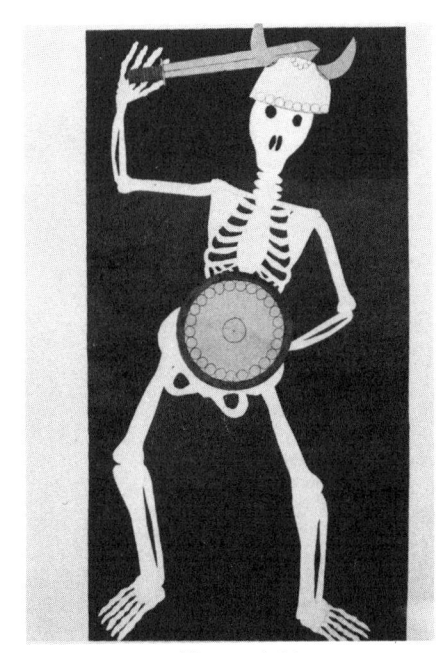

Figure 1-16

Variation:

Reproduce the entire set of bones in Figure 1-14 so students can work independently. Or cut out the bones from a stiffer paper or cardboard. Put them together with brass fasteners to make a movable skeleton.

A drawing rather than a cut-out skeleton may be done by having students follow step-by-step drawing procedures on 12" x 18" drawing paper. Bones may be labeled.

Use:

The basic names of the bones could be mastered and their use encouraged in daily conversation. "My patella hurts" or "Your cranium must be empty today" could become everyday sentences. Present the words in a spelling list, too.

2

Paper turns into many items with a little help from your friends

These lessons teach your students various methods and techniques for achieving design, depth, and expression. Included are projects on puppetry, poster making, miniature construction, collages, and many holiday crafts.

42   Turn paper into many items

light snow falling
(perforated light pictures of snowmen)

Grade Levels: 3-5   **Time Needed: 40-80 minutes**

Before You Begin:

Make one or two different snowmen and display them on a window. Shutting off the lights in the classroom produces a dramatic effect.

Objctives:

- To become familiar with the compass and its uses.
- To become aware of a use for the compass other than for drawing circles.
- To use light as another way to draw.

Materials:

- 12" x 18" construction paper, assorted colors. (NOTE: Dark colors look like night and show up the light more effectively. You may want to pre-cut the paper to fit into window-sections in the classroom.)
- pencils
- compasses

Procedure:

1. Choose a background color and use a compass to draw a snowman. Remind students to press on the point rather than the pencil when using the compass.

2. Draw three circles, being careful to leave space for a hat, scarf, boots, twig arms, mittens, carrot nose, and plenty of snowflakes to be added. (See Figure 2-1.) All drawing and erasing should be confined to one side of the paper. The other side will be the front.

3. When the drawing is complete, start the perforations. Notice that the sharp end of the compass is pointed and gets thicker farther up. If it is used very gently, the holes will be pinpoints; if it is pressed all the way

Turn paper into many items 43

Figure 2-1

through the paper, the holes will be larger. Choose one size for the holes or use a combination of sizes.

    4. Hold the paper in the lap and follow along the lines, poking holes through the pencil drawing.

    5. Be sure the holes are not poked too close together, as this will

weaken the paper and cause tearing; on the other hand, holes that are too far apart will result in difficulty in discerning details. (See Figure 2-2.) Check by holding the paper up against a window occasionally.

Figure 2-2

6. No words should appear on this drawing as it will be displayed in reverse.

Uses:

This lesson could be used for such Christmas decorations as candy canes, presents, toys, trees, stars, and manger scenes. It might also be used along with studies of the stars and planets or for exclusive compass and ruler designs. The possibilities are endless.

look, mom, hands!
(cut paper Easter rabbit)

Grade Levels: 4-5   **Time Needed: 40-80 minutes**

Before You Begin:

As spring and the Easter holidays approach, make these rabbits to use as attractive and sophisticated decorations for windows, bulletin boards, or baskets. Demonstrate making one of these little rascals while your students watch, or have them cut along with you. The hands on the rabbits are the key to their charm because they can be manipulated like real hands to hold carrots, eggs, and baskets, or even to hold hands with each other.

Objectives:

- To develop direct cutting skills.
- To encourage the total use of supplies.
- To develop individual designing within a given framework.

Materials:

- 9" x 12" pastel and white construction paper. (NOTE: White vellum is ideal for this project as it shows up marker details better.)
- colored scrap paper
- 12" x 18" construction paper, assorted colors
- scissors
- pencils
- glue
- markers or crayons

Procedure:

1. Select four sheets of the same color paper. Encourage direct cutting rather than sketching first, for most of this lesson. Before assembly make

46 *Turn paper into many items*

sure all pencil traces are erased for a clean final product. Some parts may be turned over.

2. Cut the first sheet into a basic egg-shaped body and head, fatter at the bottom and thinner at the top, using up the entire paper.

3. Use the leftover paper from the egg for whiskers and a tail. Tear out the tail to get a puffy effect and cut along the curved edges for the whiskers. (See Figure 2-3.)

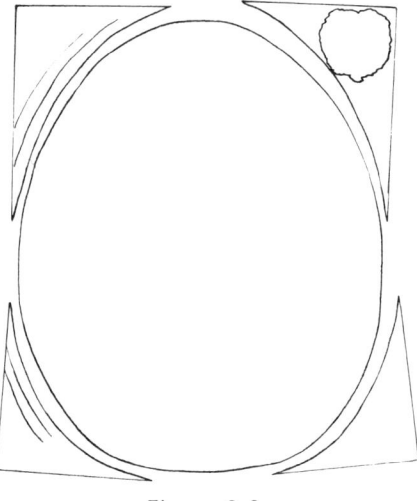

Figure 2-3

4. Fold two other sheets of paper in half to make hands and feet. (See Figure 2-4.) Use your non-cutting hand and wrist as a model to trace, making sure that finger tips are at the top of the paper. Use the other sheet to make feet with haunches. Then cut along the lines.

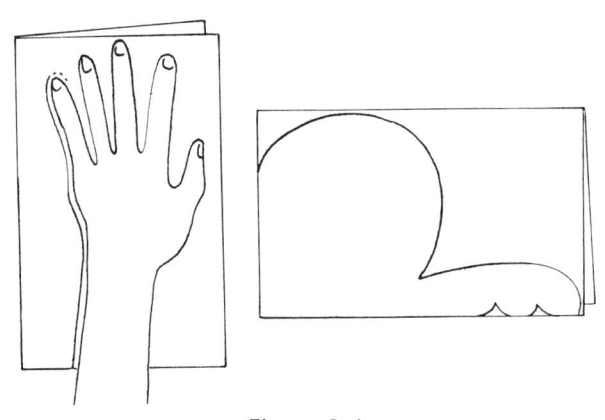

Figure 2-4

5. Fold the fourth sheet of paper in half lengthwise to make tall ears. Two different ears can be drawn and then cut out, or one can be cut double. (See Figure 2-5.)

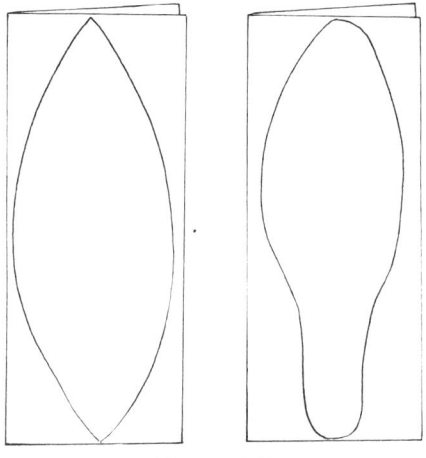

Figure 2-5

6. Give the rabbit action by placing one of each cutout hand, foot, and ear behind the egg body, and arranging the others in front. (See Figure 2-6.) Try several different actions—running, sitting, hopping—before gluing the rabbit to the background.

Figure 2-6

48   *Turn paper into many items*

7. Or, have the rabbit come forward by placing all cutouts behind the egg. (See Figure 2-7.)

Figure 2-7

8. Remember to place the hands correctly—thumbs up or down, depending on what the hands will be holding.

9. Add facial details by using markers or crayons, and glue on the whiskers (either curled up or drooping).

10. Use scrap paper for such additional details as carrots, bow ties, vests, decorated eggs, baskets, paint cans and brushes, and aprons. (See Figure 2-8.) The rabbits can now "hippity-hop" into spring!

Figure 2-8

Uses:

The rabbits may be made small to decorate the front of a card, become the border for a room decoration, or fill in small windows. Larger rabbits can cover a door or wall, sit in a chair or become the subjects of short stories and poetry.

animals can talk, too
(origami hand puppet)

Grade Levels: 3-6   **Time Needed: 120 minutes**

Before You Begin:

Make several puppets to show your students. Use animals with ears—dogs, cats, rabbits, mice, raccoons, lions, tigers, and pigs. Only the head is needed for an effective puppet, but bodies and clothes may be added for a more developed character. (See Figure 2-9.) Let the puppets talk to each other or to an audience to excite your students into making their own.

Figure 2-9

Objectives:

- To learn new terminology, such as "origami."
- To give students an opportunity to express themselves through a character or group of characters.
- To become familiar with a puppet-making technique for future use.

Materials:

- 12" x 18" construction paper (assorted colors). NOTE: 12" x 12" squares are needed, so these may be cut prior to the lesson on a paper cutter. Accuracy is important or this puppet will not work.)
- scissors
- glue
- stapler
- ruler
- pencils
- scrap paper

Procedure:

1. Cut the 12" x 18" sheet into a square and roll it over in half, corner to corner, matching the corners perfectly. Press just the center of the paper to make a fold mark; repeat the process in the other direction so that a small folded cross marks the center of the paper. (Do not fold all the way across as the unnecessary fold will cause difficulty with the final folding.)

2. Put a small pencil dot at this center cross, and fold each corner into the center, leaving the dot exposed each time. (See Figure 2-10.) After the four corners are folded in, there should be a tiny space between all the edges of the resultant triangles and no corners should be folded over each other.

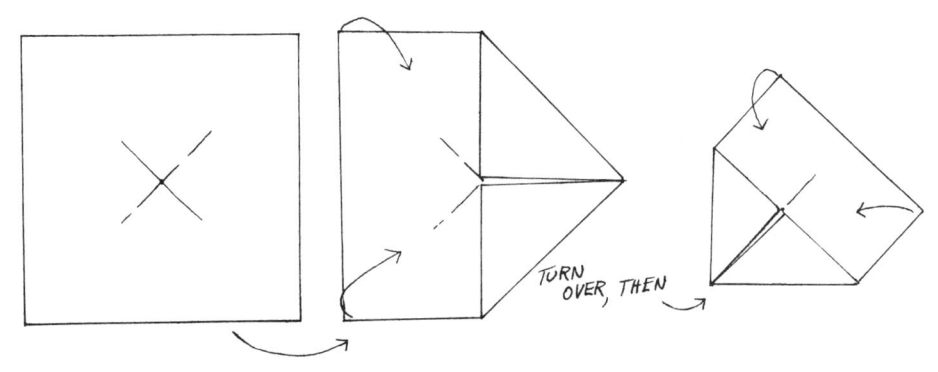

Figure 2-10

Turn paper into many items 51

3. Turn over the whole paper and repeat the same folding process, taking care to leave space by not bringing the corners exactly to the center.

4. Fold the package in half, exposing the squares on the outside and folding the triangles inside. Open it up and fold the other way to coax the paper into the proper folds.

5. Tuck your thumbs and index fingers under the four squares and open up the puppet head by pushing into the "mouth" with the fingers. Students who are able to complete their folding first may act as "helpers" for other students.

6. Staple two sections together to form a mouth that opens in only one direction. Go in as far as possible with the stapler. (A miniature stapler is helpful for this step.)

7. Fold the leftover rectangle from the original 12" x 18" sheet in half to make two ears. (See Figure 2-11.) Draw one ear and then cut two from the folded paper. Encourage using the whole paper to draw the ear.

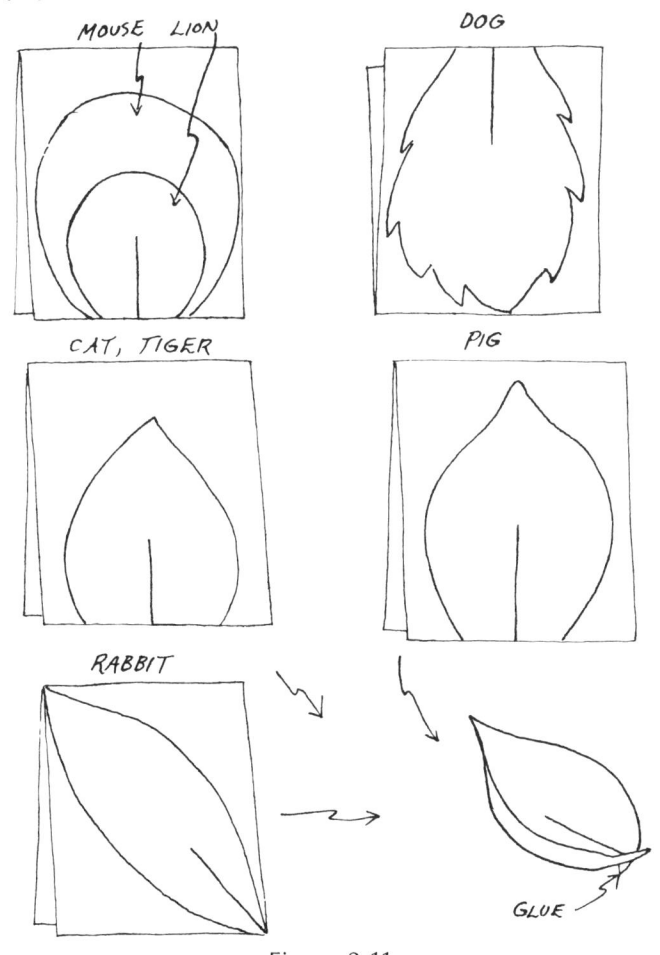

Figure 2-11

8. Cut a slice into both ears about 1" to 1½" long from the flat side or bottom. Cross over and glue each ear so that it forms a cupped shape at the split end.

9. Make sure that the mouth opens in an up-and-down direction, then glue the cut-and-glued section of each ear behind the two top corners of the puppet head. The two bottom corners can be rounded off or sliced into thin strips and curled up for the whiskers.

10. Add fringed paper around the head from the back for a lion's mane or a dog's curly hair. Fold down a pig's ears to hang over the face. Put a dog's ears on the same way and fold down, or glue them on the front of those top two corners so that the ears hang down at the sides of the face. Use different color paper for a dog's ears if a two-tone effect is wanted.

11. Add facial features with scrap paper or pre-glued tape. Follow the suggested drawings for making eyes—they are important because the mouth of the puppet is so large. (See Figure 2-12.) Make a basic white shape, an iris in color, then a pupil and reflection. Use the "fooball, baseball, and golfball" concept for the shapes and sizes to be used, but a round shape could be used instead of a football for a "wide-eyed" look. Cut the shapes out from doubled paper so that both eyes can be made at once. Coins may be used to trace round shapes.

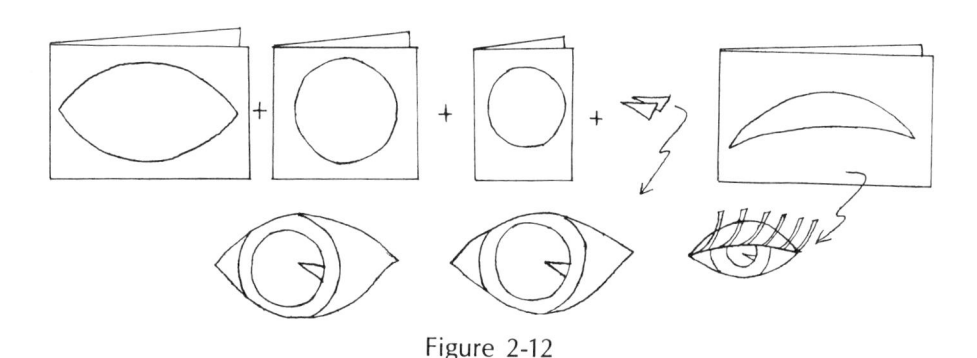

Figure 2-12

12. Make eyelids from a "football" shape cut lengthwise, and eyelashes from small strips of paper that are fringed and curled. Glue these to the edge of the eyelid, or to the top of the eye if there is no eyelid.

13. Use scrap paper to add noses, tongues, teeth, whiskers, freckles, glasses, lipstick, lollypops, carrots, and any other details that enhance the puppet's head. A pig's nose is made from folded paper. Cut two slots, insert the tabs and tape in place. (See Figure 2-13.)

Turn paper into many items 53

Figure 2-13

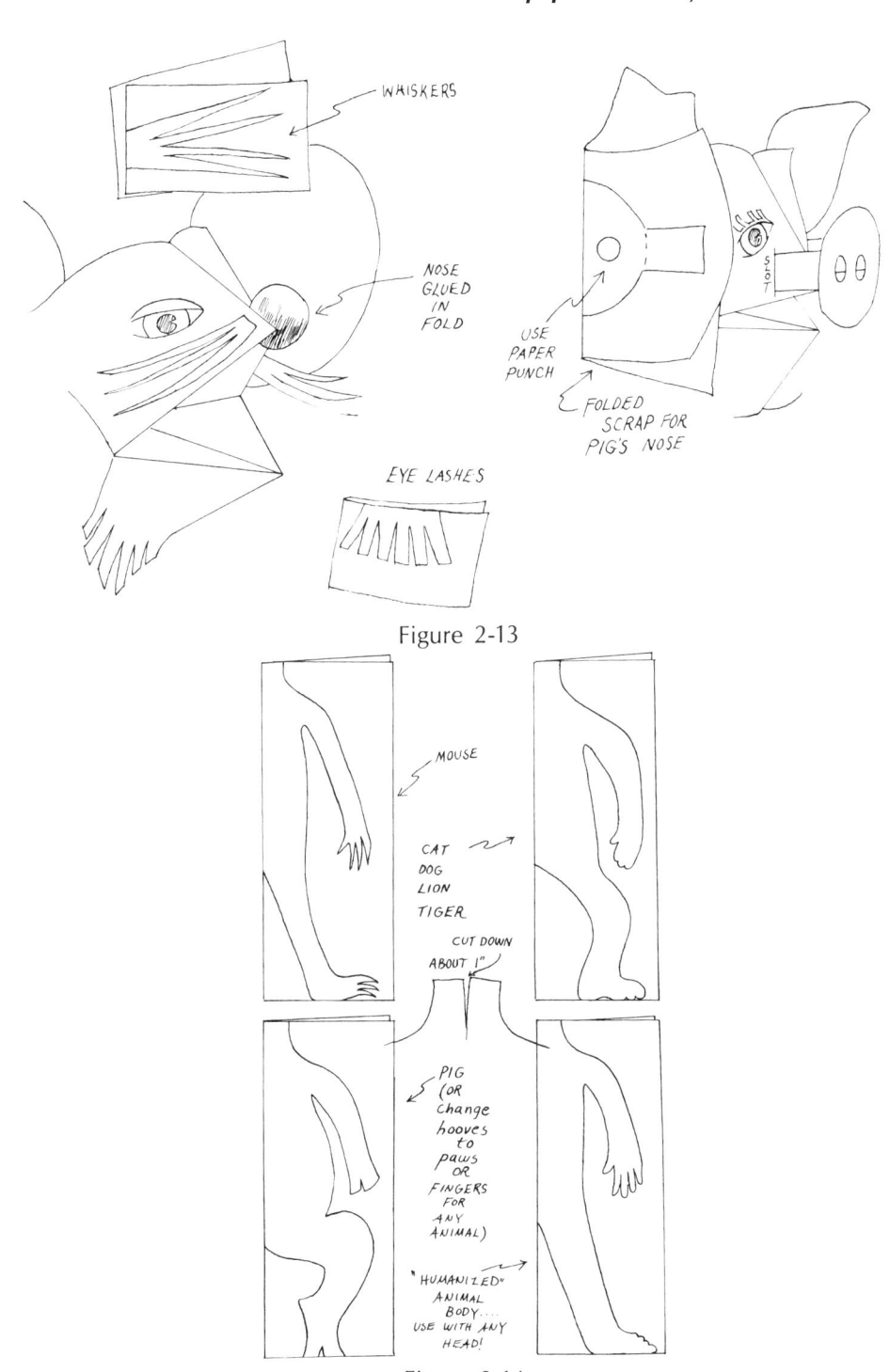

Figure 2-14

14. Make the body from the same size colored paper as the head, using the 12" x 18" rectangle folded in half, lengthwise. (See Figure 2-14.) Draw one-half of a body from the folded side, using up the whole paper.

15. Cut and then open up the body. Cut a slice down the center fold in the neck area about 1" in length. Glue this split section behind your puppet's head. (See Figure 2-15.)

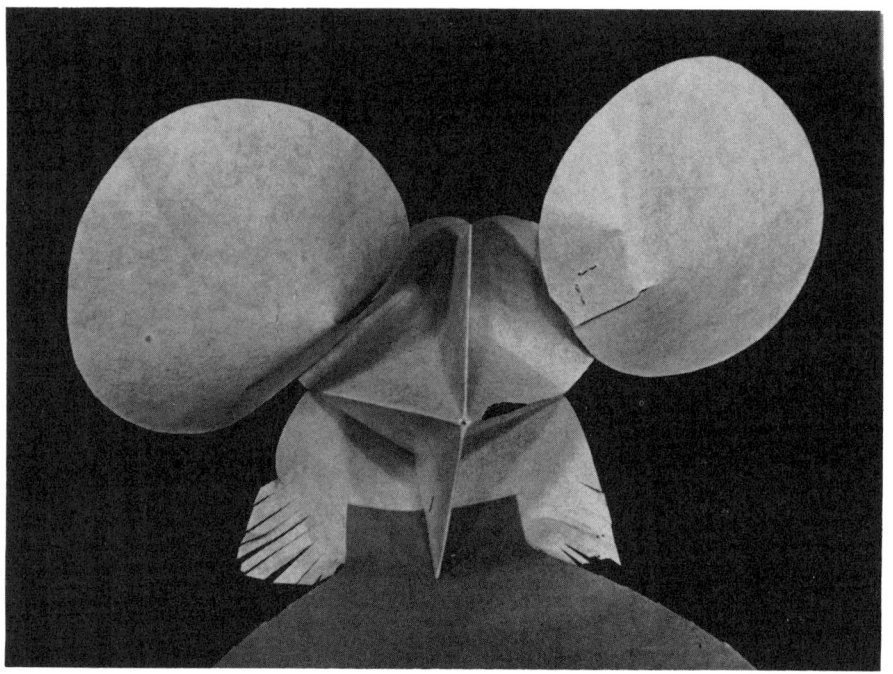

Figure 2-15

16. Make clothing either in a paper-doll fashion with tabs so that clothes can be changed, or make clothing permanent by gluing it on. After the body has been attached, lay the puppet face down, with colored paper behind the body. Trace a little bit larger around parts of the body for the kind of clothes you would like. (See Figure 2-16.) Many variations can be made from the basic drawings shown.

17. Cut out the clothes after removing the puppet and completing the shapes. Turn the drawings over and add details with scrap paper, real items, or drawing (pockets, buttons, trims, stitching).

18. Paper may be decorated by using several crayons at once to "plaid," "stripe," or "swirl" a design. Wallpaper may also be used instead.

Turn paper into many items 55

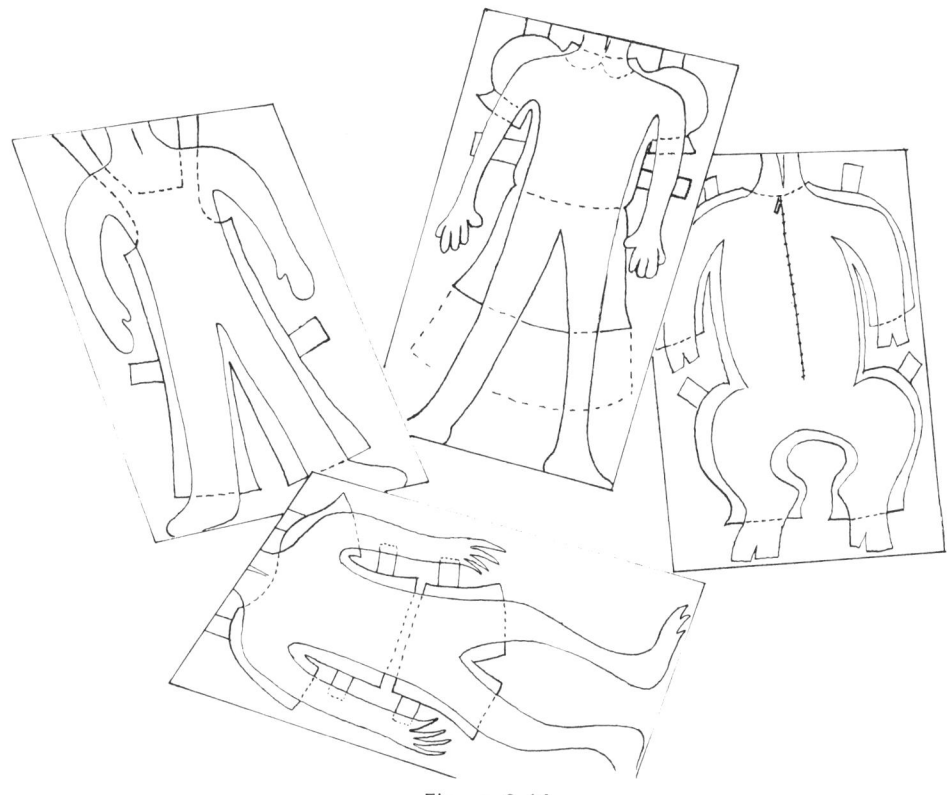

Figure 2-16

Uses:

The puppets may be used for simple dramatization by each student, and for expression of creative writing. The puppets can also be used for holiday-related activities or to study various aspects of language, health, hygiene, and other subject areas. Puppets may be made in various sizes depending on the size of the initial square. A family in different sizes (see Figure 2-9) or a whole collection of small puppets makes an interesting project.

you'll love these
(valentine cards)

Grade Levels: 4-6   **Time Needed: 40-80 minutes**

Before You Begin:

Let the students work with you as they "discover" the cutting of the valentines. After the valentine patterns have been cut, demonstrate some decorating techniques and then let the students go on their own from there to make each one in colored paper and decorate it. If your students follow directions well, start them on colored construction paper and omit the preliminary practice. There may be some mistakes, but the scraps can be used for additional decorations.

Objectives:

- To make more elaborate valentines, rather than the usual straight cutouts.
- To experiment with folding and cutting paper.
- To experience making, rather than buying, something to share with someone else.

Materials:

- 9" x 12" newsprint or manila paper
- 9" x 12" construction paper, assorted colors or white
- scissors
- crayons or markers
- pencils (optional)
- glue
- sequins, lace, doilies, ribbon

Procedure:

1. Use three sheets of newsprint or manila paper to practice. Then use the construction paper to make the finished valentines.

Turn paper into many items 57

2. Fold two of the sheets in half. Then fold back both ends to meet the middle fold. (See Figure 2-17.) From the ends, the folded sheets should look like an "M" and a "W." (See Figure 2-18.)

3. Fold the third sheet of paper in half and in half again, like a greeting card. (See Figure 2-19.)

Figure 2-17

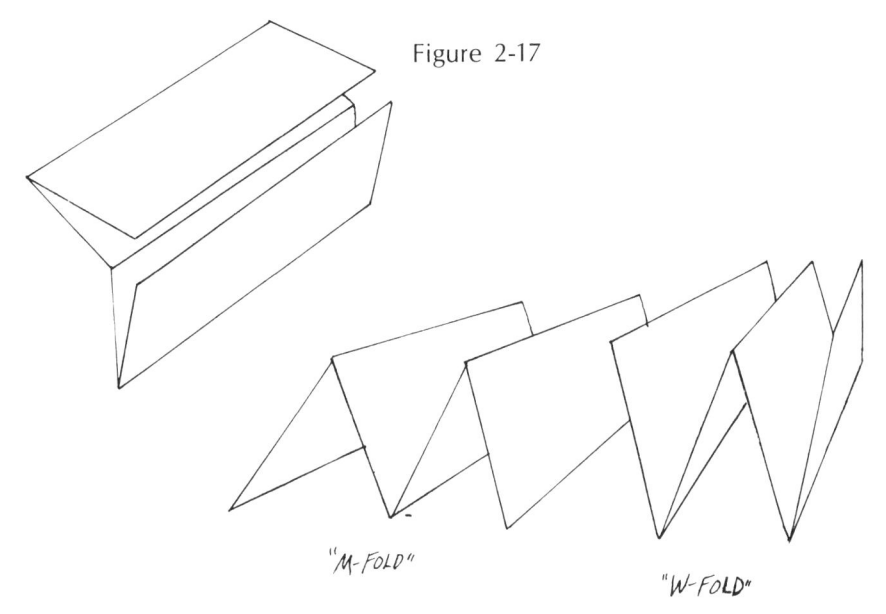

"M-FOLD"   "W-FOLD"

Figure 2-18

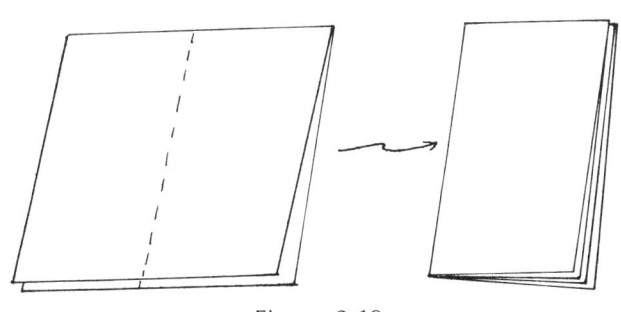

Figure 2-19

4. To make all the cuttings, follow the sketches. (See Figure 2-20.) On the side of the paper where the student holds with his non-cutting hand, tell him to check under his thumb for an "open-fold-open" or the top of the "W" fold, to make the first valentine with shutter doors. The second or double valentine is made the same way, but by holding onto the "M" side

or "fold-fold" of the next paper. He holds onto the single fold of the third paper with a double fold at the top to get the lift-up valentine. On all three cuttings, he must "cut in the air" to form the hinges. This is shown in the sketches with dotted lines. Preliminary drawing may help but try to make these cuttings without a pencil outline. In all cases, cutting starts below the thumb at the bottom corner of each paper.

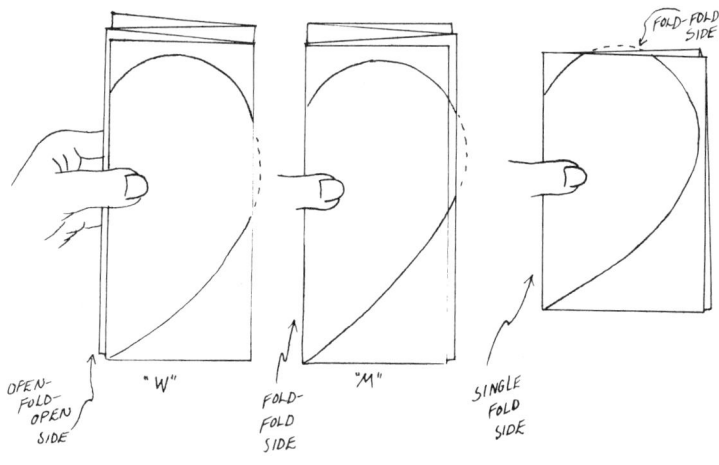

Figure 2-20

5. Cut hinged "doors" that either lift up or open from the side. Open the heart all the way and cut into one of the attached hearts. Fold the heart in half and, while holding on to the fold with the non-cutting hand, cut around the thumb in a half-heart shape. Do not cut all the way through. Leave a small uncut part to keep the door connected. Make a door that opens from the side by cutting the door open through one of the hinges. (See Figure 2-21.)

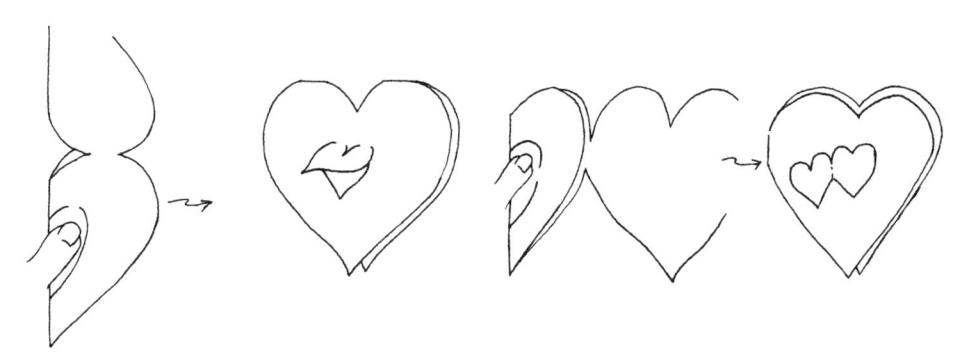

Figure 2-21

6. Finish the valentines by decorating them with markers or crayons. Slip scrap paper behind doors to color them differently from the main heart. Try gold and silver crayons on the hearts, especially if they are made from dark colored paper. (Hearts do not always have to be red!) Decorate the valentines with bits of lace, ribbon, doilies, and sequins.

Uses:

Hearts can be made larger for bulletin board displays, or as backdrops for stage decorations. They can be made extremely small and given as gifts, or pasted onto a poem to represent words. And, of course, all valentines can contain verse or sayings—but be sure to introduce a vocabulary list so that the detailed work will not be spoiled by misspelling!

60   *Turn paper into many items*

let's pitch a tent
(paper models for outdoor scenes)

Grade Levels: 4-6   **Time Needed: 80 minues**

Before You Begin:

Make samples of an army medical tent or a camping tent complete with attached canopy and campfire. The students, even those who have never been camping, will have ideas on how to finish their tents. Remind them to start collecting items for the theme they choose.

Objectives:

- To present a basic construction technique that can also be used for other projects.
- To develop accuracy in cutting and folding.
- To provide an expressive, creative outlet.

Materials:

- 12" x 18" construction paper (green and brown for military tents; orange, yellow, and blue for camping tents)
- scissors
- glue
- rulers
- string or yarn
- cardboard base
- natural materials for ground decoration (stones, sand, moss, twigs)
- small toys, dolls, animals, accessories
- netting (optional)
- material (earth colors) to cover base

Procedure:

1. Cut the desired color 12" x 18" construction paper into a 12" x 12" square. This square must be accurate. Keep the leftover 6" x 12" strip on the side.

Turn paper into many items 61

2. Fold the 12" x 12" sheet into 16 squares. Cut only on the parts of the folds marked with an "X" in Figure 2-22. Be very accurate in these steps.

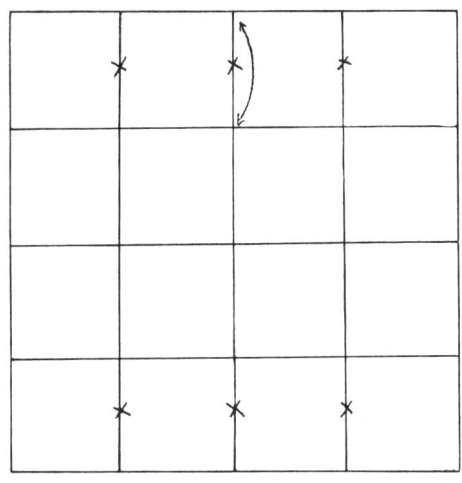

Figure 2-22

3. Glue the tent together by overlapping the two middle cut squares and then overlapping these with the two on the outside to form a "house" shape. (See Figure 2-23.) Do the same gluing on the opposite end. Line up the squares accurately, making sure the bottom edges are even. (See Figure 2-24.)

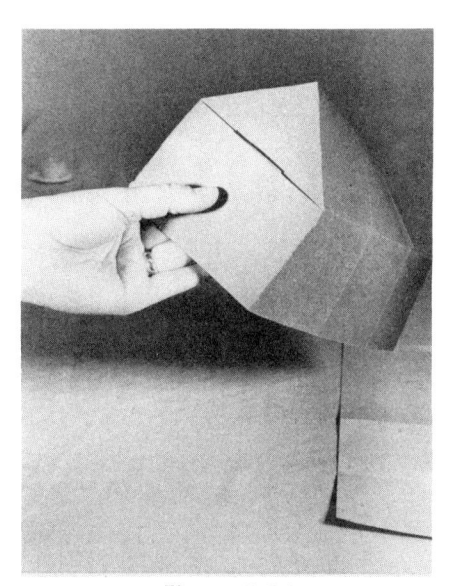

Figure 2-23   Figure 2-24

62   *Turn paper into many items*

4. Cut up the middle of one end of the tent and roll or fold back the door flaps. If this is done immediately after gluing, they will fold back easily and stay in place as the glue dries.

5. Cut windows out of the side of the tent. Use a ruler and a pencil to sketch lightly; then poke into the middle of the windows with scissors and trim them out, or leave a "flap" by cutting only three sides. Add realism to the tent by cutting net material a bit larger than the window and gluing it in place from the inside of the tent.

6. Use a leftover 6" x 9" strip in a different color for a roof and canopy. Fold the strip in half, and one half in half again, and glue this half to the top of the tent. Let the other half extend over the side to form a canopy. Prop it up by gluing on twigs or straws. (See Figure 2-25.)

Figure 2-25

7. Cut four pieces of yarn or string into one-foot lengths. Knot the end of each one with a big knot—this will hold the string inside the tent. Poke four holes into the top corners of the roof and put a dab of glue at each hole site. Thread the yarn through until the knots are pulled against the glue. Let the yarn dry in place. Do not attach the ends to the base until it has been arranged.

8. Be creative when making the base of the tent scene. Use a box lid that is painted green or brown; or cover plain cardboard with colored paper or with green or brown material. Use newspaper crumpled up under the material to form a hill at one end of the scene. Staple the material in

Turn paper into many items 63

place after wrapping it around the cardboard. Use different colors of paper or cloth to show sand, a path, a lake or grass. Mirrors for water, and stones, twigs and artificial plants can be arranged. A box lid filled wih sand will provide a realistic beach.

9. Wrap the yarn (from step 7) around twigs or toothpicks and glue into holes poked through the base. Or attach the yarn by wrapping it over the edge and taping it to the bottom.

10. Complete the outdoor scene with a campfire built from twigs and bits of colored cellophane. Arrange logs to sit on, and stones to line a path or edge a brook. Fold and tie brightly colored material with yarn to look like sleeping bags. Arrange toy dishes, utensils, food packages, dolls, a canoe, and any other camping gear around the tent. (See Figure 2-26.) Making a tent can be almost as much fun as going camping!

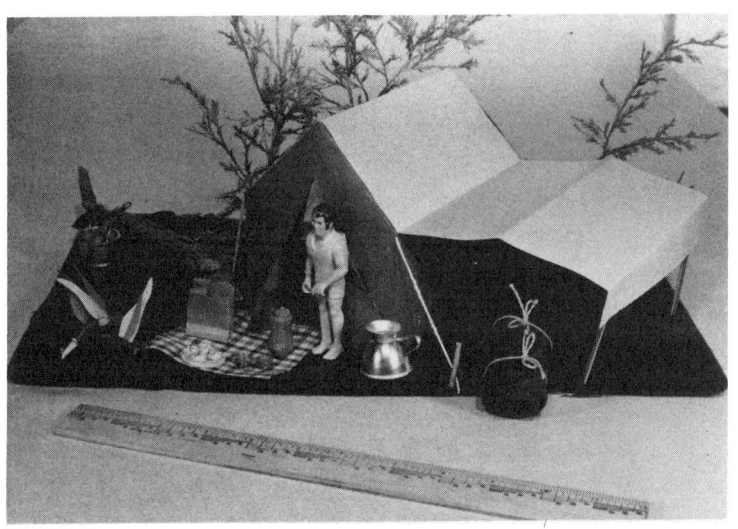

Figure 2-26

Variations:

This basic construction can become a house by adding colored paper squares and cutting windows out of the center, leaving the color as trim. Various models can be used to represent different types of houses around the world and to illustrate stories. (See Figure 2-27.) These scenes can be lit by cutting a hole through the cardboard base and placing a small bulb through the hole and into the tent or house. Tape a single socket cord in place. For a dramatic effect, set up an entire "encampment," with a tent

Figure 2-27

over each bulb in a string of lights. Twinkling lights can even be used to give the effect of camp lanterns! The basic structure can also be used as a circus tent, using colored Plasticine clay for animals and clowns.

Turn paper into many items   **65**

making a scene
(three-dimensional scenery)

Grade Levels: 5-6   Time Needed: 80-120 minutes

Before You Begin:

Discuss types of scenes that can be used for this lesson or in conjunction with other subject areas. Some examples are underwater, desert, mountain, and camping scenes. Make two or three examples to stimulate your students' interest.

Objectives:

- To use simple materials for creating a three-dimensional scene.
- To learn new vocabulary, such as "foreground," "middleground," "background," and "foliage."
- To provide practice in intricate cutting.

Materials:

- 12" x 18" construction paper (assorted colors)
- colored chalks or crayons
- rulers
- scissors
- manicure scissors (optional)
- stapler
- photos or illustrations from magazines (optional)

Procedure:

1. Choose three sheets of construction paper. One color is for the background, such as the sky and mountains, or the inside of a cave. The other two are for the middleground and the foreground. For example, if making a desert scene with mountains in the background, the colors from the foreground to the background might be green, brown, and light blue.

2. Cut strips off the short side of the foreground and middleground sheets. Make the foreground paper into a 12" x 16" sheet by cutting off a 2-

inch strip. Make the middleground paper into a 12" x 17" sheet by cutting off a 1-inch strip. The two shorter sheets of paper will be made into "frames" through which the background will be seen. (See Figure 2-28.)

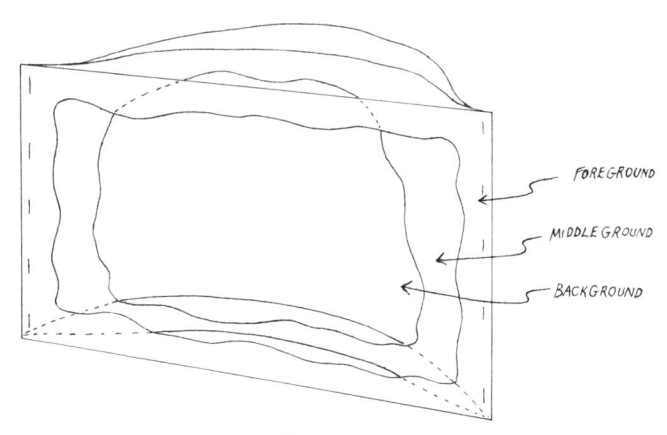

Figure 2-28

3. Each sheet is made up of the elements and objects that are needed to create the mood of the scene. Roughly plan out the scene on scrap paper; then go to light sketches on each sheet. On the foreground, for example, draw foliage and cactus, some dried bones and animal skulls, and perhaps the beginning of a path. Color in with chalk and then cut out the center area to form the frame. (See Figure 2-29.)

Figure 2-29

4. Use the middle ground to show desert sand, hills, more cactus, and an old miner's shack, making sure that the drawing forms a thicker frame than the foreground plan. Cut out the middle area, including the top which could be fashioned into clouds or flying vultures. (See Figure 2-30.)

Figure 2-30

5. Use the background to draw and color in the sky and mountains.
6. Staple the three sheets together by aligning them at both ends and using six staples along each end. This will cause the middleground and background sheets to be rounded for self-standing. (See Figure 2-31.)
7. Create a nice effect for trees or foliage by tearing, instead of cutting, the edges where trees might hang down. This technique can also be used to represent whitecaps on the ocean. (See Figure 2-32.)

Figure 2-31

8. The foreground and middleground may have objects that cross the frame opening from top to bottom, such as a lighthouse, tree, or ladder. The frame opening is cut in two sections. (See Figure 2-32 again.)

Figure 2-32

Variations:

If more depth is wanted, paper could be cut into graduated widths that vary more than one or two inches. You might also use more than three sheets. Try four or five! You could use sturdier paper or oaktag, and make the scenes larger.

Uses:

Illustrate a book or fairy tale your students have read. Or make scenes where people are more important than scenery, such as in a sporting event.

look out! I can see you
(characters with roving eyes)

Grade Levels: 5-6   **Time Needed: 80 minutes**

Before You Begin:

Show several faces you have made up that represent different types of characters. The movement of the eyes is all that is needed to excite your students and get them started. You might also display charts showing several types of facial features, such as eyes, noses, mouths, horns, ears, etc. (See Chapter 3's "Symmetrical Scaries" for ideas.)

Objectives:

- To draw facial features.
- To use highlighting and shadowing on faces.
- To learn the meaning of "vignette."
- To learn a simple animation technique.

Materials:

- 12" x 18" construction paper (assorted colors)
- 9" x 12" white paper
- crayons
- scissors
- tape

Procedure:

1. Choose construction paper according to the skin color of the face to be drawn.
2. Starting about one-third of the way down from the top of the paper, draw two shapes for eyes. These eyes should be a little larger or smaller than a quarter and could be round, almond-shaped, square, rectangular, half-moons, cat-eye shaped, etc. (See Figure 2-33.)
3. Cut out the two eyes.

70   *Turn paper into many items*

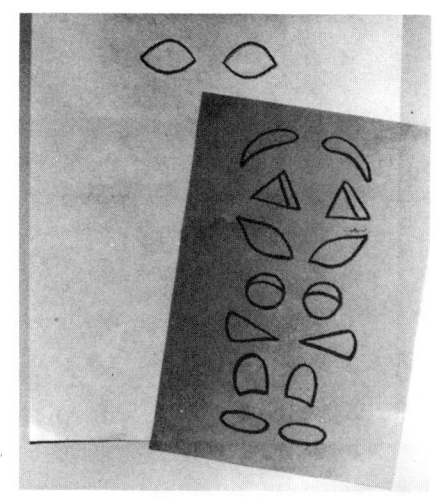

Figure 2-33

4. Use black crayon to draw a nose and mouth before drawing the final face shape. (Crayon can be erased if drawn lightly at first.) In this way, the tendency will be to draw larger rather than smaller. If the face does not fit after all the features are drawn, use the "vignette" technique of letting the drawing fade off the edge of the paper where necessary by drawing and coloring lighter near the edge. (See Figure 2-34.)

Figure 2-34

5. Use black, white, and crayon similar to the paper color to shade and highlight the face. For example, on a green witch, use the side of a dark green crayon to shade in the face, a black crayon to make shadows around the nose, under the eyes, at the sides of the face, in cheek hollows, and under the chin, and a white crayon to highlight the nose, above the eyes, cheekbones, end of the chin, forehead, and lips. Add other colors for hair and clothing, using black and white for shadows and highlights. Color the background solidly so that the face shows up dramatically. (See Figure 2-35.)

Figure 2-35

6. Take a sheet of 9" x 12 " white paper and cut off a strip about 2" x 12".
7. Cut two curved notches from both ends of the 7" x 12" remaining sheet, place it behind the eye holes, and tape it in place. (See Figure 2-36.)
8. Slip the 2" x 12" strip into the "envelope" and center it behind the eye holes. Put a black dot in the center of each hole (see Figure 2-37) and pull out the paper to complete the eyes. It is important that the eyes are completed *after* pulling out the strip; if not, they will be too small.
9. Make a pupil larger with black, leaving a bit of white as a reflection. Cats' or devils' pupils are not round, so make the proper shape. Add a colored circle around the pupil for an iris, and then add bloodshot lines if desired.

72   *Turn paper into many items*

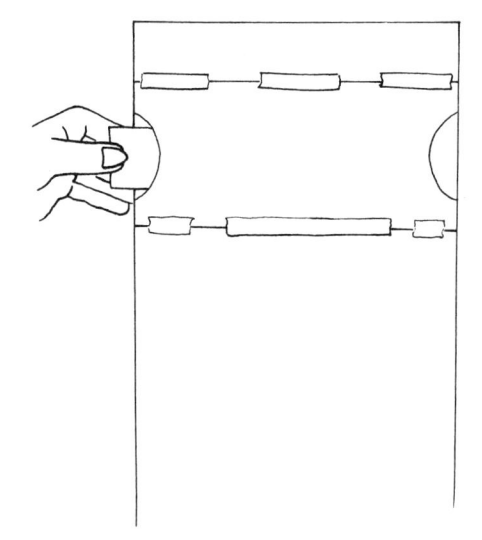

Figure 2-36

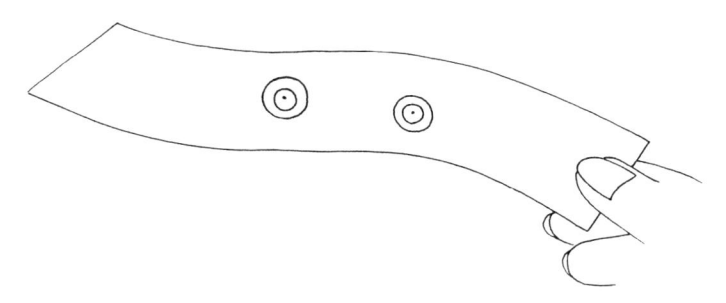

Figure 2-37

10. Add lids above the eye-shaped hole, and eyelashes, if desired. A second set of eyes can be made on the back of the eye strip, too.

11. Slip the eye strip back into the "envelope" and move the eyes up and down, back and forth, round and round!

Variations:

The faces might be cut out and added to separate bodies. Or have two or three students work together on making huge characters with bodies to display on the classroom walls.

Uses:

Decorate the classroom for Halloween with these faces. Possible characters include werewolf, vampire, Frankenstein's monster, robot, skeleton, witch, devil, jack o'lantern and goblin. Other faces could portray storybook characters, such as an Indian, ballet dancer, gypsy, hobo, angel, clown, and football player. Some examples are shown in Figures 2-38 and 2-39.

Figure 2-38

Figure 2-39

74   *Turn paper into many items*

that's strange
(distortion of a magazine picture)

Grade Levels: 5-6   **Time Needed: 80 minutes**

Before You Begin:

Discuss "distortion" and its meaning; that is, to change the usual shape or appearance. Illustrate this meaning by making faces at your students or using the words "stretching," "squashing," "separating," "reversing," "subtracting," and "changing." Relate the word to language meanings, as in "stretching the truth," "out of context," "deleting the facts." Then show a few examples of pictures you have made using the technique described here. The bizarre effect of these pictures should motivate your students to begin art distortion.

Objectives:

- To experiment with distortion, using a recognizable factor (picture).
- To develop composition through shape, line, and rhythm.
- To understand the various ways distortion can occur.

Materials:

- magazines with large color photos without advertisement or print to interfere with the picture. (NOTE: Faces of people and animals are ideal, but objects or scenes can also be effective.)
- 12" x 18" background paper (assorted colors)
- glue
- cotton swabs or toothpicks
- scissors
- pencils
- rulers
- compasses
- french curves (optional)
- scrap paper (to cover work area and to make folders for work storage)

Turn paper into many items 75

Procedure:

    1. Select a picture to work with and trim it into a "format" or shape—possibly an oval, circle, octagon, rectangle, square, or any other irregular shape. Use a ruler for straight edges.

    2. Decide how the distortion will occur in the picture. Lightly pencil the distortion on the back of the picture, using a ruler, compass, French curve, or freehand lines. (See Figure 2-40.) Check occasionally on the front of the picture to see that lines will not cut through unwanted places, like the middle of the eye, unless that effect is desired.

Figure 2-40

    3. Begin cutting, and number the pieces on the back if they are of similar shapes and sizes. If they are graduated in size, this won't be necessary. Folders may have to be made to store the work in if time does not permit continued work.

    4. When finished, arrange and distort the pieces on the background paper. (See Figure 2-41.) Distortion is created by leaving small spaces between pieces or by graduating those spaces. Pieces may be arranged in reverse or upside down. If shapes were cut out of the center of the picture, they could be replaced with the same shape from another area. (An eye might replace a mouth if circles or squares were cut out all over a face.) A small pattern of a symmetrical shape could be used. Fold the picture where the shape is to be cut. Slip the folded pattern over the fold and cut around the pattern. Repeat several times, then interchange the pieces. (See Figure 2-42.)

76   *Turn paper into many items*

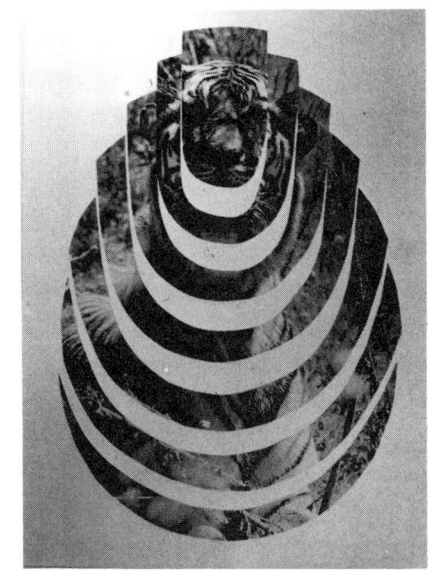

Figure 2-41

Figure 2-42

5. Create a target effect by using a compass to cover the picture with circles. Cut into the center from the edge of the circle, making an easy access to cut each consecutive ring. (See Figure 2-43.) Spin each ring slightly when placing it on the background paper, then glue the rings onto the paper. The cutting is hardly noticeable. (See Figure 2-44.)

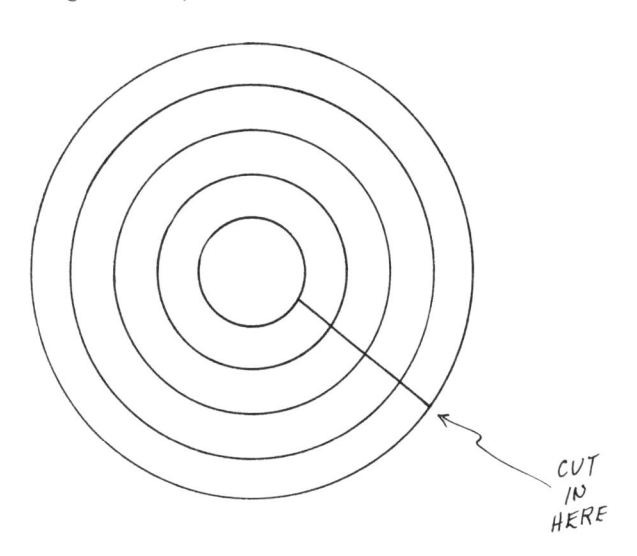

CUT IN HERE

Figure 2-43

Turn paper into many items 77

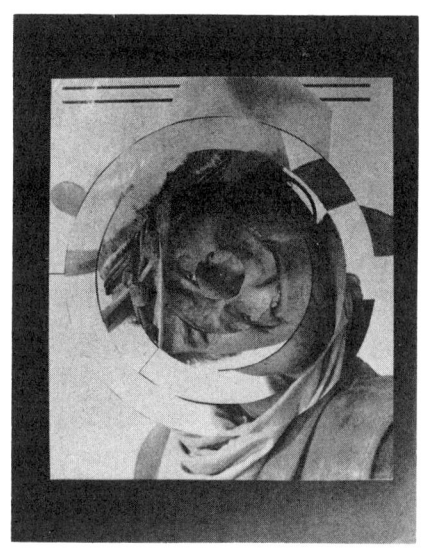

Figure 2-44

6. Checkerboard, pie shapes, random sized strips, curved strips, squares.... any pattern may be used, but make sure the whole picture is used for the distortion.

7. Glue pieces onto the background and display finished products flat or inside shallow boxes. Laminating these distortions helps to smooth out edges and enhance the quality of the picture.

Use:

These pictures may be used to encourage creative writing. Poems or short stories using a science fiction or fantasy theme could be developed by the students.

photo potpourri
(picture humor and mystery)

Grade Levels: 5-6   **Time Needed: 80 minutes**

Before You Begin:

The areas developed through this lesson are humor or "what's funny?" and the elements of mystery or bizarre associations. Most students are aware of what is funny, but have difficulty expressing it in a sophisticated way. Talk about opposites (an adult sitting in a high chair to eat dinner) or predicaments (a football player watching the football fly out of the stadium). Mystery is a little easier to express because the students can use scenery, people, and objects to show something that has already happened or will happen in the future. Bizarre arrangements of things are probably the most fun to work with as there is more leeway for creative thinking. Since no drawing is required to create effective results, this process will be fulfilling to most students. Make a few examples to show the different ways the magazine elements can be put together.

Objectives:

- To introduce new elements of expression.
- To encourage creative thinking.
- To develop observation and manipulative skills.

Materials:

- magazines (to research for pictures)
- scissors
- glue
- 12" x 18" background paper (assorted colors)
- scrap paper (to cover work area)

Procedure:

1. Look through a magazine (or magazines) and cut out interesting objects and faces. Look for a large object, face, or other background on

Turn paper into many items 79

which to arrange and glue the elements collected. Then look for other elements that tie into the background to carry out the theme, and any words (if necessary) to convey the idea.

2. Explain the process of "inventing an idea," as this might be difficult for some students. Give them adequate time to research their theme. In the examples shown (Figures 2-45 and 2-46), many different magazines were researched. After finding the watch repairman with tweezers and a strange look on his face, the bowl of soup and over-sized watch were found to complete the picture. The background picture was also the stimulus for the second example, so this will be the most important element of the arrangement. The small teeth were found in an advertisement and chosen for their tone, which matched the background. Finally, when the large tooth was found, the whole idea took shape ... a proud farm couple with their prize-winning tooth, home grown among the others of only average size! This creative process must be discussed, and students should be encouraged to help each other in researching needed items.

Figure 2-45

Figure 2-46

3. If the background has to be cut in order to slide something into or behind an area or object, be sure the cutting is accurate so that the finished product looks as if it were always that way.

4. Glue parts onto background and press under a heavy weight. Lamination smooths out the finished picture, but it is not necessary.

Variation:

A definite theme could be given to tie into a particular area of study, such as history, politics, science or different cultures.

Use:

This lesson lends itself to creative writing, with poems and short stories springing from the finished pictures.

Turn paper into many items 81

the paper connection caper
(figures from a basic pattern)

Grade Level: 6 **Time Needed: 80-120 minutes**

Before You Begin:

All children have cut paper dolls at some time during their art experiences and they may want to try doing one now from memory. After they have tried, open your "bag of tricks" and pull out one or two that you have made prior to beginning the lesson. (See Figure 2-47.) The students will be amazed that the ones you have made are connected but not the same, and they will want to learn how to do it. The trick is to "build up" all the characters into a composite for the first cutting.

Figure 2-47

Objectives:

- To develop thinking skills in the use of foresight.
- To encourage design development within a confined framework.
- To provide opportunity for detail drawing and cutting.

82 Turn paper into many items

Materials:

- 9" x 18" or 12" x 24" white vellum drawing paper
- pencils
- scissors
- markers or crayons

Procedure:

1. Fold a sheet of drawing paper in half.
2. Wrap each half back to meet the fold: this forms a "fan fold."
3. Decide what characters to draw. This fold creates four figures. NOTE: Christmas is a good theme for this lesson because there are so many figures that are appropriate: Santa and Mrs. Claus, elves, snowmen, angels, dolls, teddy bears, and soldiers. Choose four separate figures, or repeat two, or use one and three, as in Santa and his three elves.
4. To make two Santas and two wives, draw a fat Santa with a hat, a full jacket, long dress, and big boots. (See Figure 2-48.) Hinges are important for connecting the figures, so mittens, knees, boot tips, or elbows are drawn off the fold on both sides.
5. Cut out the figure. Open up the paper and refold in half so that the two figures can be completed and trimmed with scissors.

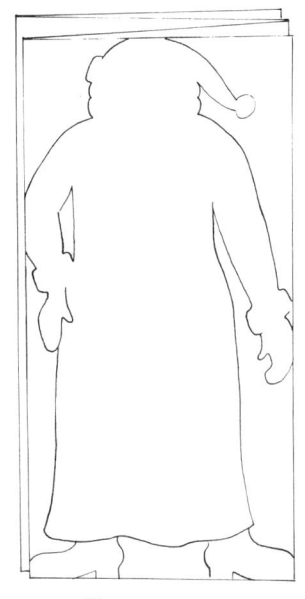

Figure 2-48

Turn paper into many items 83

6. Make Mrs. Claus by thinning the figure, making the jacket become her dress, drawing her shoes a little smaller, and taking off the hat. Be sure to leave hinges. To make Santa, change the bulky dress into a jacket and pants tucked into tall boots. (See Figure 2-49.) Again, remember to keep hinges. Boots and hands may touch—or elbows and toes.

Figure 2-49

7. Open up the paper, erase any unnecessary drawing, and finish all of the characters with markers or crayons. (See Figure 2-50.) One Santa is enough for adults—but children don't mind seeing double!

Figure 2-50

8. If you were to make a snowman plus a Santa, a small boy, and a little girl, start with a large, undefined snowman, a hat on a round head, and fat arms that go to the folded edges. The bottom of the snowman should fill the bottom edge of the paper—flat to the ground. Cut out, open up and draw each character, taking care to develop hinges between each one. The boy and girl could be started from two sections folded together. A snow-suited figure with long hair can become a boy with a trim of the hair! Santa is drawn out of the snowman, and the snowman is left.

Variations:

The characters may be associated with different holidays, such as Easter rabbits, St. Patrick's Day leprechauns, or Halloween goblins. They could also be historical—Roman citizens, Vikings, or American Indians.

Uses:

When completed, the figures can be mounted on background paper to make attractive holiday decorations or cards. Students can also complete the backs of the characters and stand them on a table to be viewed from all sides. (See Figure 2-51.) Several can be set up in a circle to make an unusual centerpiece, or displayed in a window.

Figure 2-51

say it with letters
(block letters)

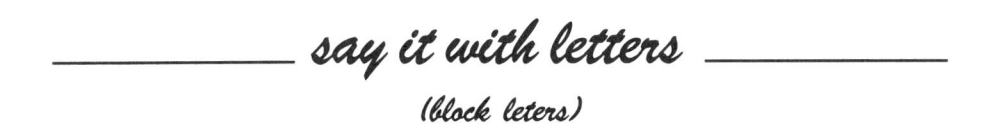

Grade Level: 6 **Time Needed: 80-120 minutes**

Before You Begin:

Show your students the letters that you have cut out using the sketches in Figures 2-52 and 2-53. Make two sets of the letters, cutting out one set and leaving the other drawn, so that your students can follow by looking at the sketch of each letter and its cut-out counterpart. Then show the students a poster you made by using an interesting saying arranged on background paper. (See Figure 2-54.) Discuss some sayings that your students may want to use. They might do some research to come up with a famous saying, or they may prefer to use a movie title, a song title, or a line from a poem. Set up "stations" with practice paper, rulers, pencils and scissors, and the visual directions for cutting each letter. To avoid having to cut the complete alphabet with students, choose and cut only the most-used letters, and then allow students to go to the stations they need to complete their individual sayings.

Objectives:

- To provide a simple letter-making technique.
- To promote the use of visual directions or plans.
- To provide a creative use of concise direction-following.
- To practice arrangement and use of color.
- To practice the use of some basic tools.

Materials:

- scrap paper (cut into rectangles)
- 9" x 12" construction paper (assorted colors)
- 18" x 24" background paper
- scissors

86 *Turn paper into many items*

- pencils
- rulers
- glue
- newspaper (to cover work area)
- pastels, crayons, colored pencils, markers, or paints
- three-dimensional objects as decoration

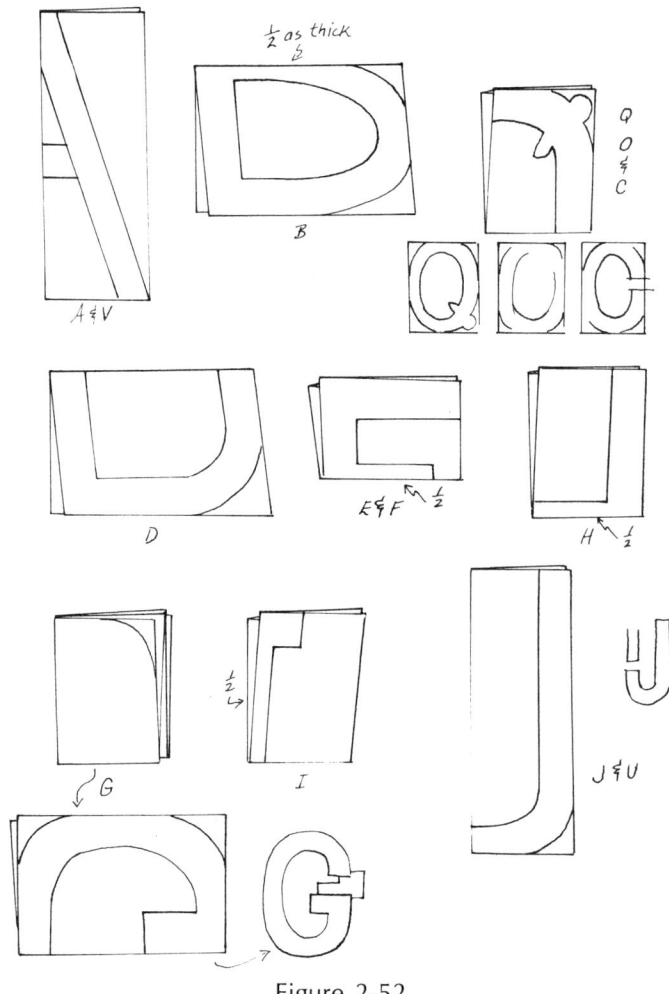

Figure 2-52

Turn paper into many items   **87**

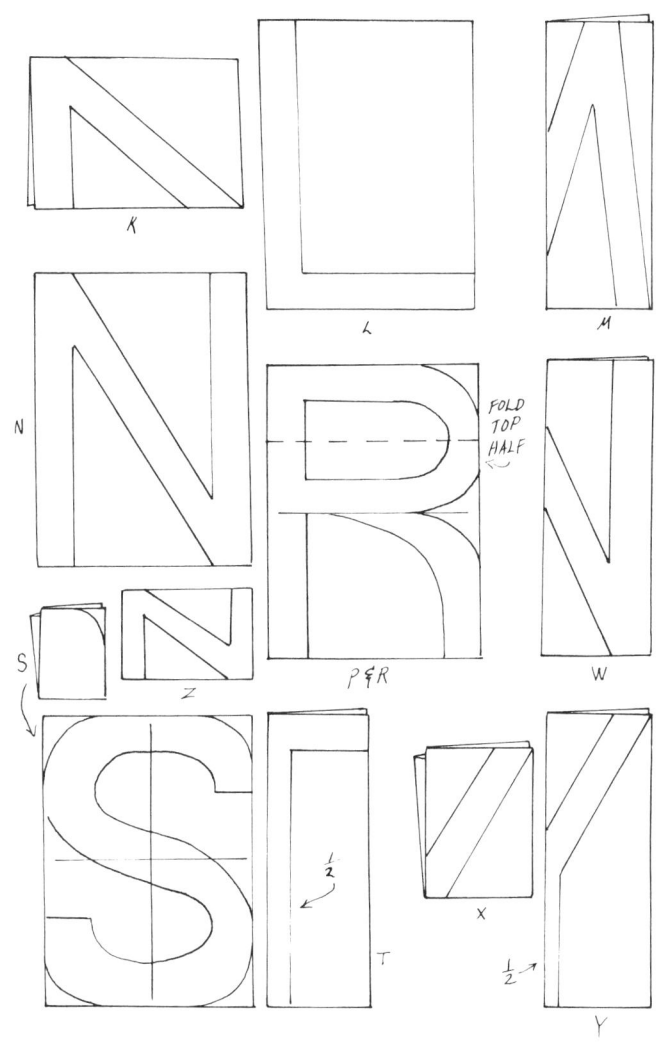

Figure 2-53

Procedure:

1. Choose a saying or title and write it on scrap paper. Some suggestions are: ME, MYSELF AND I; WHERE HAVE ALL THE FLOWERS GONE?; A HOP, SKIP AND A JUMP; SOMEWHERE, OVER THE RAINBOW; KNOCK, KNOCK! WHO'S THERE?; BUTTERFLIES ARE FREE; CHOCOLATE CAKE, VANILLA ICING. Make a required minimum number of letters for your students, to avoid one-word sayings! Use practice paper to cut the letters required for the saying before cutting them from colored paper.

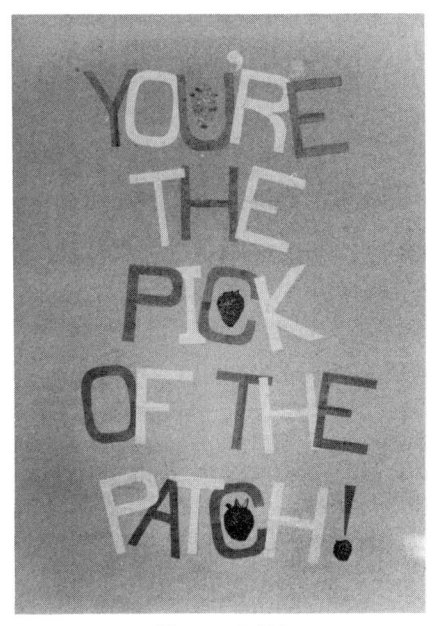

Figure 2-54

2. Take a sheet of 9" x 12" construction paper and fold it into 16 rectangles by opening up the paper between each fold. (See Figure 2-55.) If more than 16 letters are needed, fold another sheet, allowing extras for mistakes.

3. Cut along the fold lines and put the rectangles aside. (If more than one color is to be used for the letters, plan the layout on scrap paper and count how many letters are needed for each color. Some of them may also be larger than others, so cut rectangles for these.)

4. Use light pencil lines to draw the letters on the rectangles, as some of the letters will have to be used with the drawn-side up. Whenever possible, as with O,I,U,E,C, turn the letters over before gluing. If more than one of the same letter is needed, use the first as a pattern for the others.

5. When the letters have been cut out, prepare the background paper. Rub pastels on with a paper towel to create a mood, or use crayons, paint, markers, or colored pencils to illustrate the saying or to design the background. Glue on three-dimensional items, such as feathers or paper flowers.

6. Arrange the letters on the background in a pleasing pattern and glue them in place. (See Figure 2-56.) Letters may be overlapped only if they are different colors; they may also be decorated before gluing them to the background.

Turn paper into many items 89

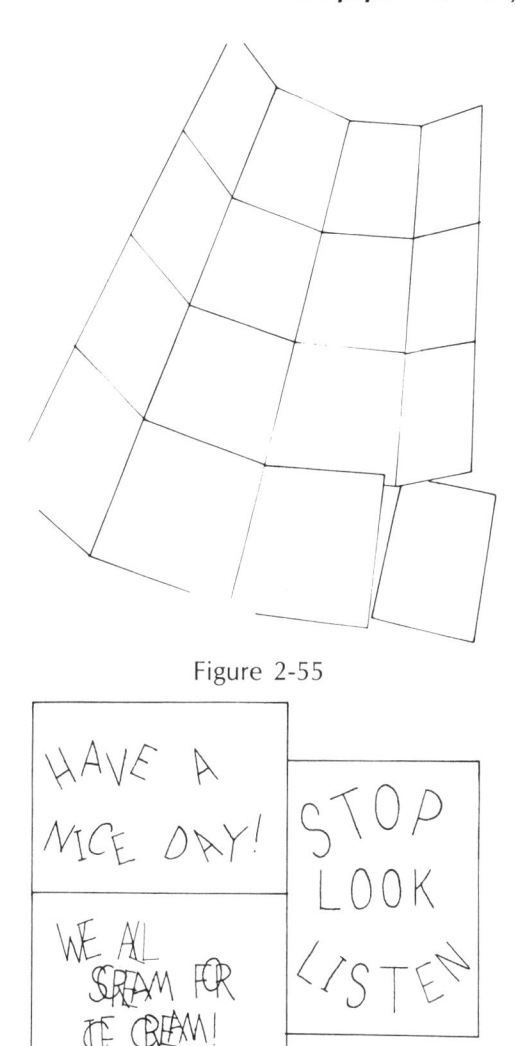

Figure 2-55

Figure 2-56

Variation:

Make a complete alphabet from small rectangles as a handy set of patterns for other projects. These could be traced onto and cut from oaktag or cardboard.

Use:

These letters can be used for many individual projects as well as for bulletin board displays and decorations.

3

Print and repeat for good times and good things

Printing can be quite interesting if you do not have to drag potatoes into the classroom! The lessons described here are based on repeats that occur by folding, rubbing, making cardboard printing plates, and using paint, crayons, charcoal and clay.

pussy willows in a pot
(fingerprints)

Grade Levels: K-3 **Time Needed: 40 minutes**

Before You Begin:

Have the children closely examine real pussy willows, noticing where the "cat's paws" or buds are located on the stems. (Each bud becomes a yellow flower in the spring.) Demonstrate the cutting of several simple vases from folded paper, then make a few branches on the background paper with crayon. Show how the fingertips are used to print the buds. (See Figure 3-1.)

Figure 3-1

92   Print and repeat

Objectives:

- To introduce symmetry.
- To be aware of the parts and purpose of a vase.
- To provide a simple means for realistic expression.
- To be acquainted with pussy willows.
- To present a simple painting technique using fingertips.

Materials:

- 12" x 18" construction paper (assorted colors)
- 4½" x 6" construction paper (assorted colors)
- paste
- crayons
- white and black poster paints
- sponges
- spoon
- pussy willows
- one or two flower vases

Procedure:

1. Talk about the main parts of a vase: the "mouth" or opening at the top to put in water, flowers, or plants; the "neck" to hold up the stems and branches; the "belly" to hold the water; and the "foot" on which the vase stands.

2. Fold a sheet of 4½" x 6" paper in half lengthwise and hold on the fold with the non-cutting hand. Leave a flat "foot" at the bottom of the paper near the fold, and cut half of a vase from the rest of the paper. The possibilities are endless. (See Figure 3-2.) Use the names of the body parts as you demonstrate several vases—remind students that they need make only one half of the vase.

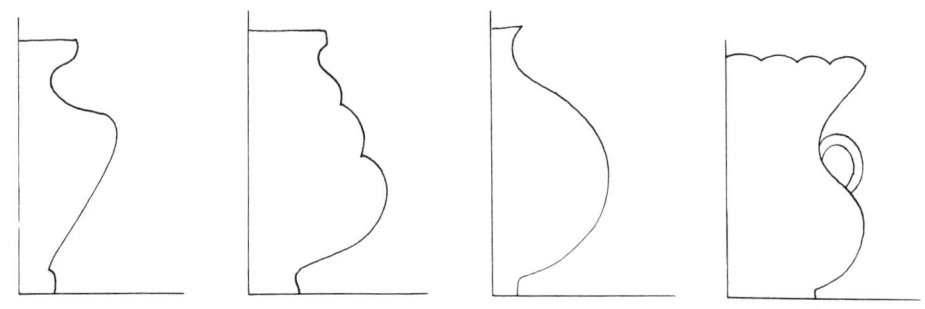

Figure 3-2

3. Open the vase and paste it along the bottom of a 12" x 18" sheet of paper. (Leave plenty of room for pussy willows.)

4. Decorate the vase with crayons.

5. Using brown crayon, draw in a few branches. (Look at a real pussy willow to see the direction.) Add a few details, such as little nubs where the buds will grow and a few tiny leaves.

6. Mix a bit of black paint into the white to make light gray (it should be of a creamy consistency). Spoon a dab of paint onto a dampened sponge and press the paint with the back of the spoon to push it into the sponge.

7. Press the fingertips of one hand onto the sponge and print each cat's paw on the branches. Use the thumb for larger buds at the bottom of the branches, and the little finger for the tiny ones near the tips.

Variation:

The same technique can be used to print flowers using several colors. Have the students turn their papers as they print so that the finger pads are applied in a circular manner around a center for each flower.

Use:

The finished pussy willow paintings provide a basis for creative writing. Write down the verbal compositions of younger students and attach them to the finished pictures.

94   *Print and repeat*

symmetrical scaries
(easy Halloween drawing and printing)

Grade Levels: 3-6   **Time Needed: 40 minutes**

Before You Begin:

Discuss "symmetry" with your students, and ask for examples of some familiar symmetrical objects. Bodies and faces, which are the subject of the lesson, should be mentioned. Demonstrate a few Halloween bodies and faces by drawing on only one-half of the paper with black crayon, folding the paper over, and rubbing with a pencil to make the other half appear. This printing technique will work nicely if your students are not too confident in their drawing. Symmetry enhances even simple drawings. The subject matter for this lesson is quite appropriate in that mistakes and errors can be used to become monster faces and bodies.

Objectives:

- To be aware of a new way to draw—by drawing less.
- To understand symmetry.
- To add a new dimension to drawing by developing facial and body characteristics in detail through experimentation.

Materials:

- 12" x 18" white or manila drawing paper (white vellum is expensive but provides excellent prints)
- crayons
- pencils

Procedure:

1. Fold a sheet of paper in half lengthwise, and draw half of a face or body with a black crayon. Be sure to start at the fold. (See Figure 3-3.) NOTE: If a heart-shaped head is made by mistake, turn it into Dracula's hairline by adding another line above it to complete the top of the head. (See Figure 3-4.)

Print and repeat 95

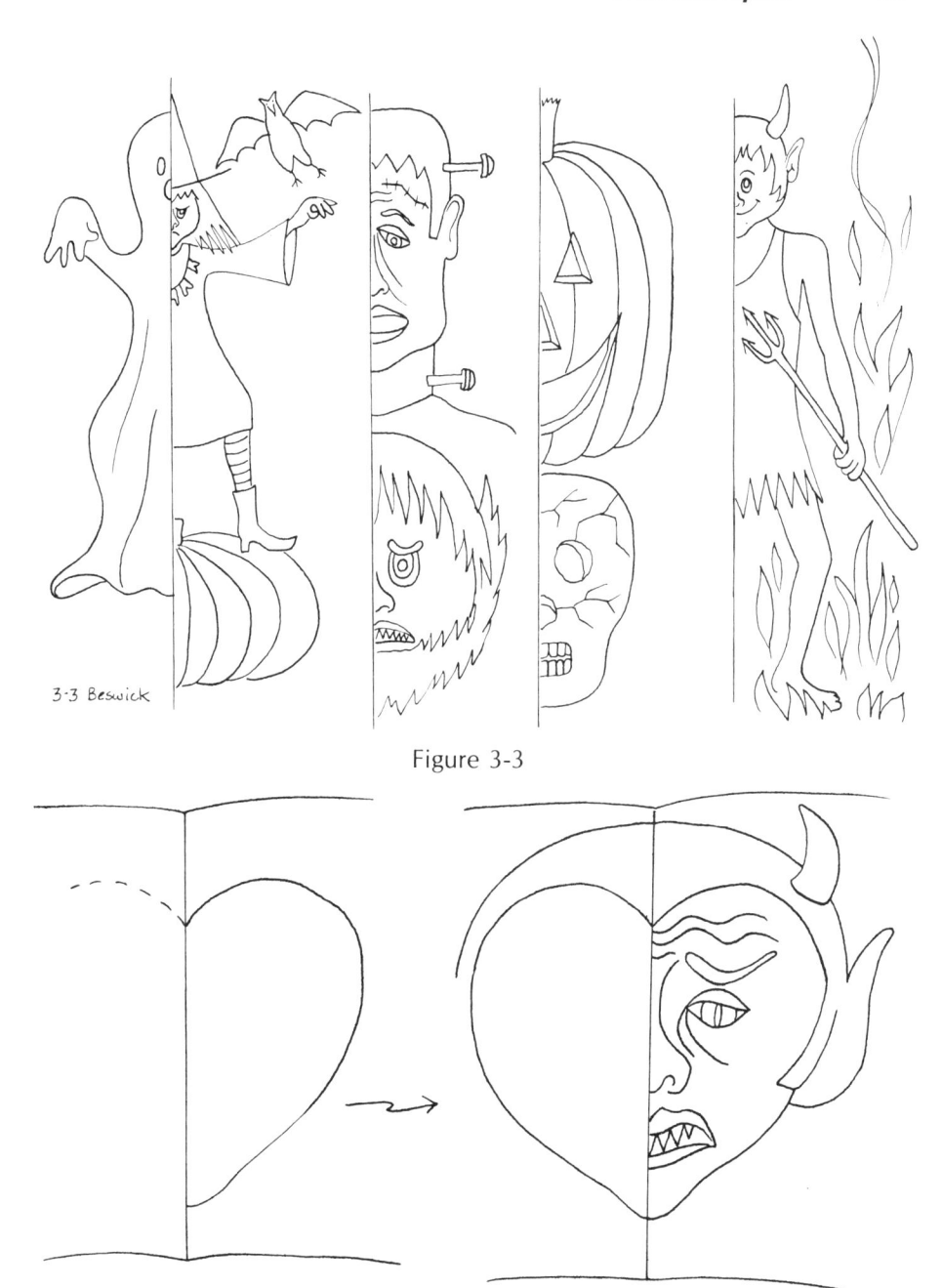

Figure 3-3

Figure 3-4

2. Draw some things away from the fold, such as an eye, and connect some things to the fold, such as half of a mouth. (See Figure 3-5.) Make sure that half of the nose is drawn close to the fold.

Figure 3-5

3. Make a body by drawing only half of the body. Start straight out and down from the fold for the head, and draw only one arm and one leg.

4. Refold the paper so that the half-drawn figure is inside. Stand up and rub all over the back of this drawing with the side of a pencil. If the image is too light, rub harder, or go over the original half with more black crayon and rub again. (See Figure 3-6.)

5. After rubbing, go over the light image *carefully* with black crayon. It is important that the reverse image be exactly the same as the original.

6. Color the picture and the background. If something special, such as a scar on one side of the face or a moon behind the bat's wingtip, is wanted in the picture, add it *after* the whole drawing is finished; otherwise, there will be two scars and two moons!

Figure 3-6

Variations:

Several drawings can be stapled together under a cover to form a holiday coloring book for younger children.

This lesson can be used for other holidays, such as Christmas or Valentine's Day. Your students might want to try drawing toys, elves, or fancy hearts. But if they are not confident in their drawing, the Halloween theme is ideal and will result in effective "scaries."

Another variation is to let your students create a scene on larger paper. They fold wherever they want a character. Several vertical folds can be used to make a monster lineup—with various bat and pumpkin folds and a few cats and goblins thrown in for good measure.

98 *Print and repeat*

___ and NOW ... in the center ring ___
(charcoal circus printing)

Grade Levels: 3-6   **Time Needed: 80 minutes**

Before You Begin:

Everyone loves a circus, and this lesson will help reinforce that feeling because everything drawn is doubled. One clown gets a twin, one dancing horse turns into a team, and one tiger poised on a stool becomes double trouble! Use symmetry to develop a circus motif by rubbing one half of the drawing onto the other half of the paper. Make up a few examples with the paper folded both the long way and the short way.

Objectives:

- To develop drawing skills through copy work.
- To increase good color sense and good coloring skills.
- To provide a simple means of expression through symmetry.
- To encourage composition development.

Materials:

- 12" x 18" white vellum drawing paper or newsprint. (NOTE: Both vellum and newsprint make a nice, crisp print, but newsprint is more economical.)
- 12" x 18" construction paper (assorted colors)
- pencils
- charcoal sticks or pencils
- erasers
- rulers
- oil crayons or crayons
- pictures and books showing circus activity, animals and acts

Procedure:

1. Cut the vellum or newsprint down to 11" x 17" before drawing so that it can be mounted on colorful construction paper.

2. Fold the paper in half. "The tall man" or a giraffe might be better drawn on a lengthwise section, while an elephant on a box fits nicely on a wider area. (See Figure 3-7.)

Figure 3-7

3. Begin the drawing using *light* pencil strokes so that mistakes can be erased easily. Remember that if a pencil is used, copying over any tiny details will be impossible since the charcoal makes thicker lines. Therefore, draw large and fill in the available space. NOTE: For a more fluid drawing, start with charcoal.

4. Draw half of some items on the fold. (See Figure 3-8.) Draw other items away from the fold. These latter items will be doubled.

5. When the half-drawing is finished, refold the paper and rub the drawing onto the other half of paper with the side of a pencil. Treat the finished rubbing carefully to avoid smearing.

6. Complete the drawing with oil crayons. Use a protective paper over part of the drawing to prevent smearing while coloring. Pale colors are very sophisticated with the charcoal outline, especially on newsprint paper, but bright colors might be better to carry through the circus theme. Stay inside the charcoal outlines for each color and neatly organize the coloring directions in each area. The finished drawings will create a fabulous show on a bulletin board or display area. (See Figure 3-9.)

100   *Print and repeat*

Figure 3-8

Figure 3-9

Variation:

This printing technique can be used for a variety of subject areas, such as science, poetry, or holidays, but the "twin" theme should be used for full effectiveness.

Print and repeat 101

please repeat yourself
(bas-relief crayon rubbings)

Grade Levels: 4-6   **Time Needed: 120 minutes**

Before You Begin:

Make an example of the "plate" or designed cardboard and demonstrate how the raised surface will yield prints when rubbed with the side of a crayon. Explain bas-relief at this point as a design that is slightly raised away from the main surface. Your students can find many examples of bas-relief around the classroom: heating grate designs, wall surfaces, tile patterns, and switch plates. Explain that "bas-relief" is pronounced like the sound a lamb makes. Show arrangements of designs that can be used—either symmetrical or asymmetrical—and explain the difference.

Objectives:

- To be aware of basic principles of art: shapes (common and unusual), organizaion of space (positive and negative), color and its use in an overlapping manner, composition and arrangement.
- To reinforce cutting skills and neatness.
- To introduce new vocabulary: bas-relief, plate, print.

Materials:

- 9" x 12" oaktag or cardboard
- 6" x 9" oaktag or cardboard
- 9" x 12" construction paper (assorted colors)
- scissors
- pencils
- rulers
- compasses (optional)
- glue
- crayons without paper wrappers

Procedure:

1. Use the 6" x 9" sheet and draw both objective (recognizable) and non-objective (unrecognizable) shapes. Be sure the shapes are simple and no more than one inch in size. Try squares, circles, triangles, fish, hearts, arrows, flowers, or odd shapes.

2. Cut out each shape and use as a pattern to make several of each. (See Figure 3-10.) Remember that some shapes can be cut in half or traced several times.

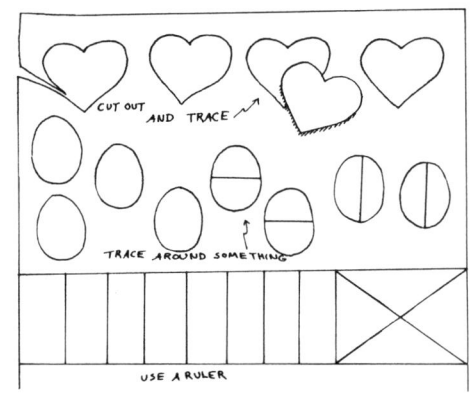

Figure 3-10

3. Center and arrange the shapes in a compact design on the 9" x 12" sheet. Do not overlap any shapes and do not extend the design to the outside edge of the cardboard; leave some room at the edges for the final composition.

4. Glue the pieces down on the cardboard by laying them upside down, one at a time, on scrap paper and applying a thin layer of glue with a finger. Keep a damp rag handy for wiping glue off the fingers. The result is a printing plate. (See Figure 3-11.)

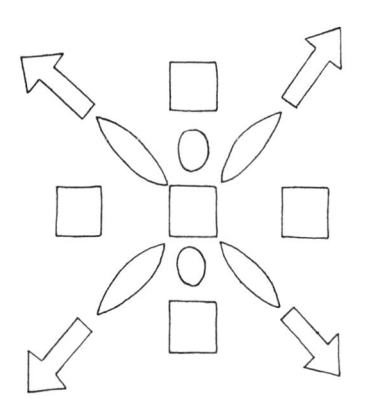

Figure 3-11

5. When dry, overlay the plate evenly with a 9" x 12" sheet of construction paper. Use the sides of peeled crayons and apply several layers of color, rubbing just beyond the pasted shapes. Be sure the papers do not slip. Color in one direction and form an outside shape wih your crayons just beyond the pasted shapes: an oval, a circle, a rectangle, a square, a diamond. Use two or three colors on top of each other, starting with light colors on light paper and ending wih dark colors. Wih dark paper, start with dark colors and end with light. Gold or silver as a final layer is an effective finish.

6. Frame each print by drawing decorative lines and small designs around the colored shape with the end of the crayons used for the rubbing. Leave the outside border of colored paper empty as a final frame. (See Figure 3-12.) Each finished rubbing is called a print.

Figure 3-12

Variations:

Enlarge the size of the plate to 18" x 24" and imagine the size of the prints you can make! Use the plate to make two or three prints, moving it slightly each time, and changing colors. Or print several times from a smaller plate to form an arrangement on larger paper, overlapping some of them.

Uses:

The lesson can be used to research certain areas of study, such as hieroglyphics, Indian symbols, mathematics, and science. The technique can also be used to make holiday or birthday wrapping paper.

104   Print and repeat

didn't I just see that?
(carbon paper designs)

Grade Levels: 5-6   **Time Needed: 80 minutes**

Before You Begin:

Show your students the various folding possibilities to get symmetrical, finished drawings in different formats. (See Figure 3-13.) The folding and duplicating of an idea (or half of one) presents an exciting finished drawing because of the magic of symmetry. A reflection in water, a collection of items or "twins" make excellent themes. The process always works, and even your less able drawers will have successful results. After

Figure 3-13

seeing the simplicity of this technique and a few finished examples, the students should be ready to begin.

Objectives:

- To develop drawing skills.
- To present a new drawing technique.
- To develop coloring sense and skills.
- To encourage thinking ahead and planning.
- To provide opportunity for experimentation with composition.

Materials:

- 8½" x 11" carbon paper. (NOTE: Any size will do, but drawing paper must be the same size.)
- 8½" x 11" white vellum drawing paper
- pencils
- colored pencils

Procedure:

1. Place the carbon paper and white vellum together, with the carbon side against the drawing paper, of course!

2. Fold the two papers either the long or the short way with the carbon paper inside so that the desired finished effect will be accommodated. *NOTE:* Students should be encouraged to draw directly, but the carbon *can* be removed while preliminary drawing and erasing occur. Then reinsert the carbon.

3. Bear down with the pencil to insure an even, dark transfer of the drawing. The subject matter may be varied to cover objects, scenes, animals, and people. NOTE: No writing of any kind should be done on the original drawing because one side of the drawing will be reversed. If letters or words are absolutely necessary to the design, slip in a piece of scrap paper to blot out the area being drawn on.

4. After the sketch is completed, remove the carbon and examine the finished double drawing. Be critical about the drawing and remove parts or add things that are necessary to make a more pleasing composition. For instance, a "spotty" drawing can be brought together by adding large objects or areas behind the floating items.

5. Use colored pencils to finish the drawing. Be neat and color in one direction in each area. (See Figure 3-14.)

106 *Print and repeat*

Figure 3-14

Variation:

Draw a larger picture by using several sheets of carbon paper along with a larger sheet of vellum. You can then fill in the symmetrical designs with paint.

Uses:

The subject matter might be confined to a particular study or holiday or theme, such as jungle animals, plants, or household objects. The lesson could also be used to create symmetrical designs to use as decorative borders for areas in the classroom.

stamp, stamp, stamp
(clay presses)

Grade Levels: 5-6   **Time Needed: 120-160 minutes**

Before You Begin:

Explain to your students that they will be making a permanent stamper or press. This stamper will be designed on its flat surface so that, when fired, it can be used to print the design on clay—or even on cookies! Make a few presses prior to the lesson to show the different ways designs can be organized on the clay surface. Designs may be "objective" (recognizable things like fish or flowers) or "non-objective" (arrangements of shapes). (See Figure 3-15.) Tell the students how the presses will be used to print medallions, necklaces, and key chains, or picture frames and plaques. (See Figure 3-16.)

Figure 3-15

108   Print and repeat

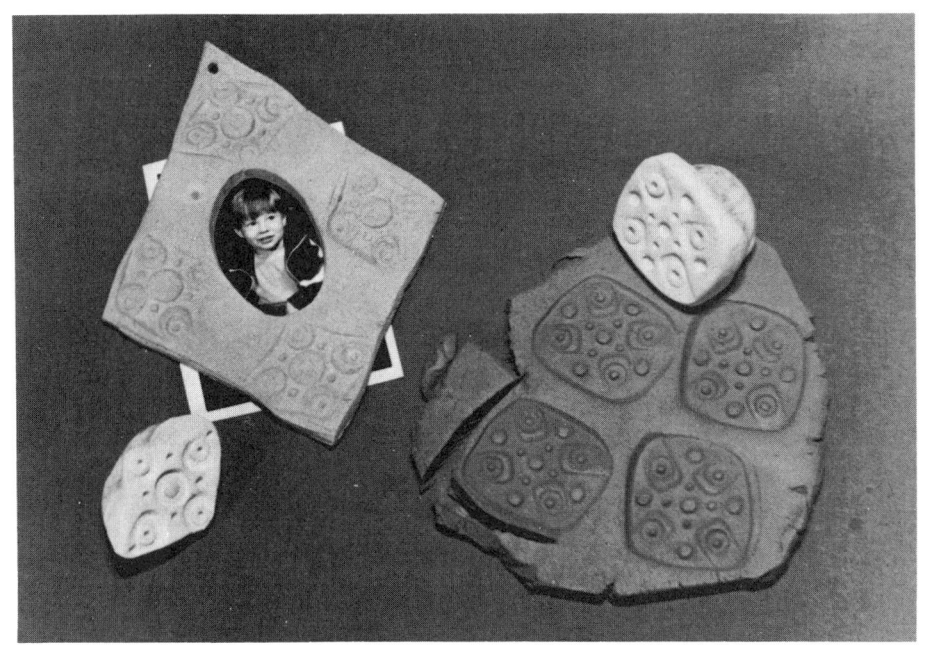

Figure 3-16

Objectives:

- To provide an opportunity for self-expression in clay.
- To present new ways to use common objects as tools.
- To introduce new terminology: press, fired, kiln.
- To develop manipulative skills in both two-dimensional and three-dimensional areas.

Materials:

- clay. (Each student needs a golf-ball-size piece of clay to make a press. More clay is needed to use the fired press.)
- a kiln
- wet sponges
- newspaper to cover the work area
- "tools" (tongue depressors, popsicle sticks, spoons, forks, butter knives, old toothbrushes, few wooden cotton swabs stripped of cotton, nails, screws, bolts, paper clips, and any odd objects which, when pressed into clay, will leave an impression)
- rolling pins or heavy wooden dowels (chair rungs are perfect)
- rulers or flat sticks

- liquid shoe polish (assorted colors)
- soft cloth
- pin backs
- ribbon or yarn
- glue

Procedure:

1. Prepare the clay by adding water with a sponge so that it is pliable. Press a thumb into the clay ball, squeeze a few drops of water from the sponge into the hole, and then work the clay until pliable. NOTE: Too much water added to the clay will make it unworkable, and it will be lost on the hands and the newspaper. Throw the clay down hard onto the newspaper-covered table a few times. This is called "wedging" and should consolidate the clay and water more evenly and rid the clay of any air pockets that might cause it to explode in the kiln, sometimes damaging surrounding pieces. Too much wedging will dry out the clay and the process must then be repeated. NOTE: Another way to avoid this catastrophe is to raise the temperature of the kiln slowly, keeping the air vent open throughout the firing, and thus allowing moisture to escape gradually.

2. Roll the clay ino a ball between the palms of the hands. Do not use the newspaper surface for this as it will continue to absorb water out of the clay and make it dry again. Put the ball down on the table and pinch it halfway down between the thumb and the side of the index finger. It should be a comfortable and substantial grasp as this will be the permanent "handle" for the press. (See Figure 3-17.) If the clay splits during this step, add more water and wedge it.

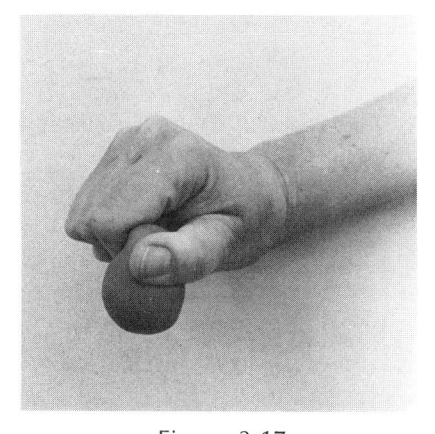

Figure 3-17

3. Hold the handle and gently tap the bottom of the ball into a flat surface which should have a thickness at the outside edge in order for the press to work effectively. Make sure the tapping is done evenly and straight down onto the table so that the clay does not split around the edges.

4. The final shape may be a circle or an oval, or it may turn out to be irregular. Coax it into a square if desired, by tapping the four sides and then retapping the press to flatten the bottom. Again, if any splitting occurs at any stage in this process, it is because the clay is drying out. Add more water, work it into the clay, and start again.

5. Press the "tools" gently into the flat bottom of the press to form designs or objects. Do not draw on the clay as this produces burrs that will show up when the press is used later on. Use an extra slab of clay to experiment with the tools and develop a design. Remember that all areas pressed *in* on the stamper will yield areas that stick *out* on the final clay jewelry or plaque. See Figure 3-18 for examples of fish scales pressed in with a popsicle stick; raised scales are produced on the final product.

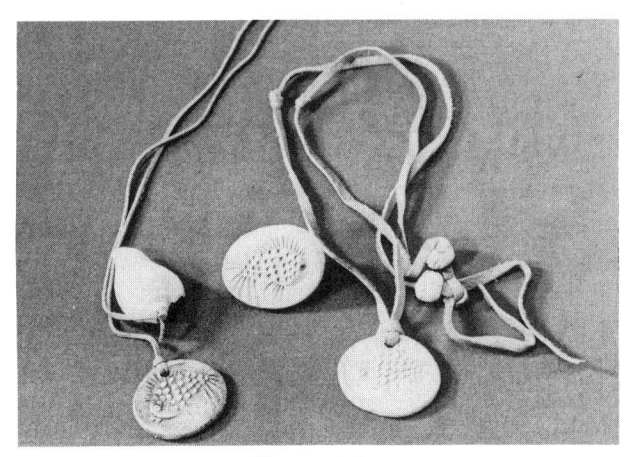

Figure 3-18

6. Scratch identifying initials into the top of the press and thoroughly air-dry the press.

7. Place the dried press in the kiln for firing.

8. To use the fired press, prepare more clay as described in step one. Roll out the clay with a rolling pin, using two rulers or thin sticks on both sides of the clay to roll against and make an even thickness of clay.

9. Press the stamper into the flattened clay to make several medallions or pins. Cut out each print with the tip of a butter knife, cutting straight down and a little to the outside of the design. Wipe the edges gently with a dampened sponge.

10. Drill a hole through the top with a cotton swab stick so that ribbon or yarn can be inserted for a necklace. (See Figure 3-19.) Make sure the hole is big enough because clay shrinks as it dries and is fired.

Figure 3-19

11. Fire the pieces in the kiln, then stain with liquid shoe polish, which will produce a glossy patina if rubbed with a soft cloth. Add pin backs, key chains, or ribbon. Braided yarn makes a good hanging for medallions.

Uses:

Plaques and mirror or picture frames are done in the same manner. The slab that is formed by rolling the clay may be used in its natural shape or cut into a particular shape by using a paper pattern. Cut out the center for a mirror or photo but remember to allow for shrinkage. Pictures and mirrors can be glued in place after firing and staining and a bit of wire can be cemented on as a hanging device.

The fired presses can also be used to stamp designs on cookies. Just be sure the cookie dough is the "roll out and cut" type. These cookies make great Christmas, Valentine's Day, or birthday gifts.

Another use is as decoration on soft clay pots or dishes. Or try using the press on paper or cloth with paint or ink. Greeting cards, writing paper, wrapping paper, and border designs can be printed by making a "reverse" press from Plasticine clay. Follow the same procedure to make the press, then make a print on the flat surface from the original press. Use waterbase paints on a sponge as a stamp pad to make prints ... but print gently.

One point to remember is that the press is permanent and can be used endlessly. When the paint has been used, the presses take on a interesting hue and are attractive artifacts in themselves when displayed collectively.

4

Draw out your students' talents

Most children want to draw but become disinterested if, by their own standards, their attempts fail because the drawings do not look cute, funny, pretty, or realistic. The following lessons develop self-confidence by presenting ways to draw realism, cartoons, and pretty pictures — all with guaranteed success.

grow potted plants
(simple plant drawing)

Grade Levels: K-2   **Time Needed: 40 minutes**

Before You Begin:

Your students will probably grow seedlings in the classroom in the spring. But seeds take a long time to grow, especially when youngsters are watching and waiting for the first sign of green to break through the soil. Why not have your students draw what they think might happen when those seeds finally *do* pop through and start to grow? Have some sample drawings to show what can be done.

Objectives:

- To encourage creative thinking and drawing.
- To learn new vocabulary: ellipse.
- To draw a three-dimensional object using a simple technique to obtain realism.
- To reinforce coloring, cutting, and pasting techniques.

Materials:

- 12" x 18" drawing paper
- crayons
- colored scrap paper
- scissors
- paste
- a clay pot

Procedure:

1. Use a black crayon to draw a clay pot. Start at the bottom of the paper. (See Figure 4-1.) The top opening of the pot is a "squashed circle" or an ellipse. To demonstrate the drawing, use the same size paper as your students are using. They will then be able to imitate your proportions more easily.

114   **Draw out talents**

Figure 4-1

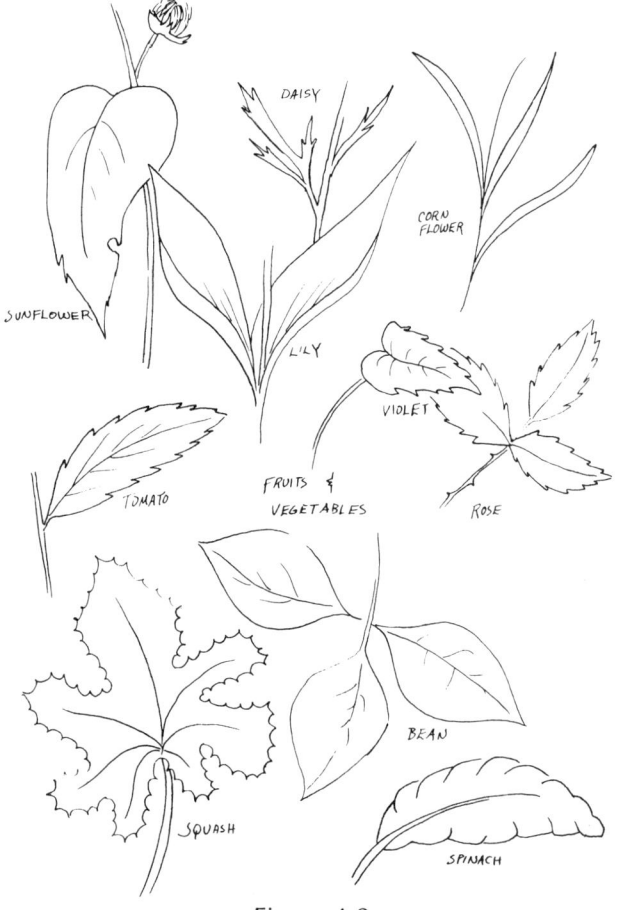

Figure 4-2

2. Discuss ellipse and show the real pot to the students. Tip it so they can see the round opening change to an ellipse.

3. Use a brown crayon to put a little dirt in the pot. Color the rest of the pot orange if it is to look like the original—or make it any other color.

4. Begin making plants using crayon, scrap paper, and paste. Observe plants to get ideas of leaf shapes or look at several pictures or sketches of different kinds of leaves. (See Figure 4-2.)

5. Cut and paste the flowers or vegetables to the plants after the stems and leaves are drawn. (See Figure 4-3.) Encourage your students to fill the paper with their plants.

Figure 4-3

Uses:

Tie this lesson into a project on plant observation. If your students are starting a plant from a seed, have them keep a record of its growth by drawing a series of pots on a large sheet of paper and recording what they see at certain intervals. If the students are growing different kinds of plants, the individual records can give all the students a chance to examine and recognize the differences.

scribble scrabble

(a drawing game or test)

Grade Levels: K-6   **Time Needed: 20-40 minutes**

Before You Begin:

Have your students begin immediately or demonstrate the procedure to them. There is no risk of the students' copying your examples as no two drawings will turn out alike.

Objectives:

- To encourage creative thinking and drawing.
- To provide a free framework for involvement and fun.
- To physically or mentally "loosen up" students.
- To test thinking and drawing skills.

Materials:

- drawing paper (any size)
- pencils or magic markers

Procedure:

1. Take several sheets of paper. Then choose a partner.

2. Make a quick scribble on the paper; it can be any kind of line, composed of curved, straight, jagged, or wiggly parts, but lines should not cross each other. Keep lines simple at first.

3. Exchange papers and complete the scribble. Look at it from different angles and add on to it, turning it into whatever is "seen." It may look like a whole object or part of something so big it won't even fit on the paper! (See Figure 4-4.) The example shows different drawings derived from the same scribble. Students will show some interesting things about themselves and their interests through these drawings.

Draw out talents 117

Figure 4-4

4. Make more creative drawings by using more involved scribbles composed of several components. (See Figure 4-5.)

ENCOURAGE DRAWING QUICKLY!

Figure 4-5

Uses:

Collect the finished drawings and use for cartoon development or creative writing. You might want to confine the drawings to things that are appropriate for a particular holiday or area of study. A particular sketch may be used for cartoon development or enlarged for coloring or painting. If all scribbles are on small paper, each student could make up his or her own sketch book by stapling the sheets together and displaying them on a bulletin board. (See Figure 4-6.)

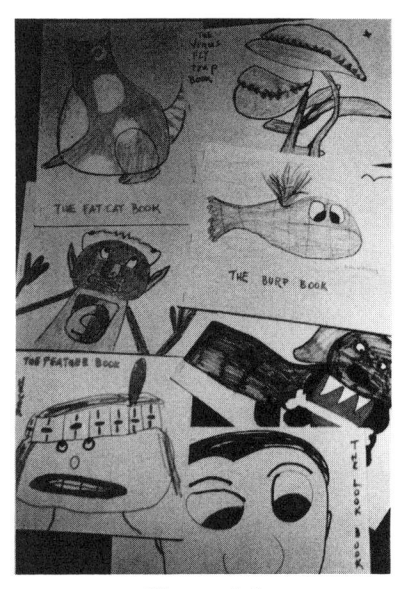

Figure 4-6

To use this technique as a "test" or evaluation of your students' drawing, thinking, and coloring skills, you may want to make up a stack of scribbles prior to the lesson. There should be enough so that each student can draw four or five. Let them "take what they get" from an upside-down stack, doing one at a time to completion.

Use a marker pen to make the lines and have students complete the drawings using crayon to finish the line drawing and color in the sketch. This enables you to "read" how the students used the line in their drawing. Have students sign their drawings on the back only. At your leisure, go through the drawings and divide them into categories. These will depend on the age level of your students. Some might be: Humorous, Original, Cute, Bizarre, Romantic, Ugly, Well-Executed, Unfinished, Careless Coloring, and Careful Coloring. They will reveal groupings of students and also your artistically gifted students.

if you laugh, I'll cry
(facial expressions)

Grade Levels: 3-5   **Time Needed: 80 minutes**

Before You Begin:

Explain to your students that only simple lines are needed to show expression and that these expressions can work for both people and animals. (See Figure 4-7.)

Figure 4-7

Objectives:

- To become aware of and draw different facial expressions.
- To develop drawing and coloring skills.
- To become acquainted with some basics of cartooning.
- To provide an outlet for individual creativity.

Materials:

- white vellum drawing paper. (NOTE: Paper size depends on the circle pattern size used for the faces. Paper cups or plastic lids make

good circles. Since eight circles are needed with room around each one, a 3½" circle needs 12" x 18" paper, and a 4" or 5" circle needs 18" x 24" paper.)
- pencils, erasers
- cups or lids to make circles for "Button Art"
- circle patterns
- colored pencils
- flat buttons or coins
- fine marking pens

Procedure:

1. Use a paper cup or plastic lid to trace eight circles on the paper. Make four in a row, leaving room around each circle for further drawing. Do each expression and have students follow along with the steps. For easier demonstration, work larger.

2. Trace around a button or coin for the nose in the center of seven circles and near the top of the eighth one. Then add the eyes and different expressions to each one in steps. (See Figure 4-8.) Students may choose to draw in any circle and may tilt their paper or turn it upside down to do some of the faces. NOTE: Avoid making too many teeth because this will give an ugly look to the face; keep them large and few and color spaces between them for a more youthful look. Color in the eyes and open mouth with pencil or marker. Be sure the coloring is done carefully and in one direction, staying within the lines. Keep the eyes close to the nose and not too tiny; if eyes are located too far from the nose, the cuteness of expression will be lost.

Figure 4-8

3. Demonstrate details to make each face become a different animal or human character. (See Figure 4-9.) Notice that some of the original

Figure 4-9

drawing (either the circle shape or parts of the expression) may have to be erased, as in the case of the little girl's head or the rabbit's teeth. Students may want to develop a theme by making a family of humans or animals, or perhaps a football team.

4. Add words or conversation between characters with "balloons." The talking balloon can point down above the speaker's head or it may point toward the mouth from either side. (Balloons should not be connected to the speaker's mouth.) The thinking or dreaming bubbles should float up from the head topped by a cloud. In both cases, print the words horizontally. Use pencil first so that any errors can be corrected before using markers. *Then* draw the balloon or cloud around the words.

5. Color sparingly on completed drawings. Use fine marking pens combined with colored pencils.

Variation:

Choose one favorite expression and draw it on a circle pattern that can be made into a button. (See Figure 4-10.) The face can utilize the whole circle, or another smaller circle can be drawn inside so that the space around it can be used for additional drawing or words. These

122 *Draw out talents*

Figure 4-10

buttons are inexpensive and a small price to pay for a permanent piece of art. All information for "Button Art" plus a ditto for running off the circle patterns can be obtained by writing to:

>John F. Kennedy Center
>Work Experience Program
>1411 Oakland Drive
>Kalamazoo, MI, 49008

Use:

Remind your students to use their knowledge of expressions in other areas, such as reports, posters, illustrations of stories, and book reports. Point out that regardless of the head shape or the kind of nose that is drawn, the eyebrow location and configuration sets the mood, along with the mouth. Students can then shift these expressions to people's faces more readily.

Draw out talents 123

scissors sillies
(trace-around cartoons)

Grade Levels: 3-6   **Time Needed: 40 minutes**

Before You Begin:

"Let's pretend that our scissors can move, make noise, and even bite! They might become human or animal, so what parts do you think would be the eyes, mouth, legs? Open the scissors, turn them around, add another pair. What do you see?"

Show a few prepared examples to let your students see how scissors can take human or animal form. (See Figure 4-11.) Give your students free rein in coming up with other good ideas.

Figure 4-11

Objectives:

- To develop drawing skills.
- To encourage the use of common contours for visual expression.
- To develop creative thinking.

Materials:

- 9" x 12" or 12" x 18" white drawing paper
- scissors
- pencils
- colored pencils

Procedure:

1. Place a pair of scissors on the drawing paper and examine it in different positions while opened and closed. Think of the parts that are missing to complete an animal or human character. Perhaps a second or third tracing of the scissors could be used to develop a monster, or maybe parts of scissors could be added. Several separate tracings can be used to develop many characters in different positions.
2. Trace around the scissors carefully, eliminating any parts that are not needed.
3. Add the additional elements needed to complete the cartoon.
4. Use colored pencils to carefully color in the character.

Variation:

This lesson may be done with all sizes of scissors and with other common objects that can be laid flat and traced, such as a stapler, a tape dispenser, pliers, and a hammer. French curves are very stimulating for this lesson also. The monsters, sea creatures, and funny faces that result are endless.

it won't rub off on me
(polyethylene sheeting and crayons)

Grade Levels: 3-6   Time Needed: 80 minutes

Before You Begin:

Talk about a possible theme that might be tied in with a particular area of study. Jungle and domestic animals, monsters of the sea, or the circus are terrific themes for this lesson. You might show your students how the marker and crayons will be dramatically affected by backing a finished drawing on various colored backgrounds. This should help them get some ideas about the color schemes they would like to use and even help with subject selection.

Objectives:

- To be aware of a different art medium.
- To present an opportunity for creative expression.
- To see the effects of overlaying colors.
- To perfect coloring skills.

Materials:

- polyethylene sheeting
- 12" x 18" or 18" x 24" construction paper (assorted colors)
- 12" x 18" or 18" x 24" newsprint paper
- marking pens (black or dark colors)
- crayons
- pencils
- stapler
- paper towels
- research material

Procedure:

1. Cut the plastic sheeting into rectangles that will fit nicely on 12" x 18" or 18" x 24" background paper. Or cut the plastic a bit smaller so that a

border will form when it is stapled into place. An alternative may be allowing students to cut a circle, oval, or other shape to accommodate the subject they choose.

2. Select a theme and sketch directly on the sheeting with a black crayon or make the sketch on a piece of newsprint paper and place it under the plastic. Trace the sketch with crayon and erase any errors with paper towels. Remember to "zero in" on the subject rather than make an all-encompassing scene. A cougar on a rock is more effective if the rock is just indicated at the bottom, with the cougar taking up most of the drawing space. (See Figure 4-12.) Encourage copy work (not tracing) from magazines, calendars, and pictures. Keep a file for this purpose. (Once a child has drawn a rabbit from a research picture, he will be able to draw one again from memory.)

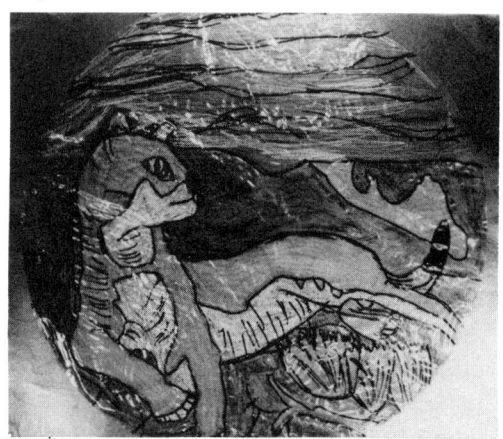

Figure 4-12

3. Use a black or dark marking pen to outline the whole sketch so that it has a coloring book effect. Run all lines off the edge of the plastic so that there will be spaces to fill in with crayon. When the ink is dry, erase all excess crayon.

4. Use crayons to color in any direction and even in different directions in separate areas, but organize your use of crayon, as every crayon stroke will become apparent when the picture is mounted on colored paper. Circular coloring may be done in round areas like the sun or a flower center; short strokes might be done in grassy areas or on animals. Use some of the marking pen techniques shown in the front-matter, Figures A-1, A-2, and A-3. All areas should have some coloring, either solid or textured. Try shading by using black lines to darken, for example, the underside of a shark. (See Figure 4-13.) Apply the black strokes on top of the gray crayon. Remember that the back of the drawing

Draw out talents 127

Figure 4-13

will be the front. Look occasionally to see how colors are developing on the other side. When the coloring is finished, choose the background color. Try several to see which best enhances the drawing. Two or more colors may be used by cutting or tearing and overlapping paper to make up the background size.

5. Place the plastic sheeting on the background paper with the drawn side down, to protect the picture from smudges and fingerprints. Staple in a few places around the edge to hold the picture in place, and set up an art exhibit of unusual pictures.

Uses:

This lesson lends itself nicely to various holiday decorations and makes attractive Christmas pictures and designs. Halloween character faces, studies of island or Indian cultures or even King Tut's tomb, as well as circus life, might be subject areas to be explored with this unusual technique. (See Figures 4-14 and 4-15.)

Figre 4-14   Figure 4-15

getting into things
(perspective)

Grade Levels: 3-5   **Time Needed: 80-120 minutes**

Before You Begin:

To get the most out of this lesson and your students, do the lesson with the students in step-by-step fashion on a paper that is larger but of equal proportions. The youngsters will be amazed at the way the picture begins to look more and more realistic at each point and will eagerly try to match your drawing as they go along. Discuss *perspective (three dimension: height, width* and *depth),* and as the lesson progresses, discuss other new words which you will list on the chalkboard.

Objectives:

- To understand and be able to draw three-dimensional pictures.
- To develop new vocabulary: picture plane, perspective, eye level, horizon, horizontal, vertical, perpendicular, parallel, vanishing point (v.p.), three dimensional, height, width, depth, vertical, diagonal, converging.
- To develop an awareness of perspective in everyday living.
- To develop drawing skills in a realistic direction.

Materials:

- 12" x 18" white vellum drawing paper
- pencils
- rulers
- erasers

Procedure:

Follow through the entire lesson yourself and become acquainted with the vocabulary and its relationship to perspective drawing. Then teach your students these basics of perspective.

1. The location of the vanishing point is very important in explaining the total perspective concept, so experiment first! It looks confusing, but

the process for realistic drawing will become matter of fact, after this lesson, for both the students and the instructor.

Explain that *perspective* means drawing things smaller as they go farther away from the *picture plane,* or the shape of the paper. This can be done by using something called a *vanishing point,* or the place where your eyes can no longer see on earth. Obviously, you can see as far as the sun or a star—but on earth, you can see only as far as the curve of the earth. This point is called your vanishing point. Another way to explain this is to imagine you are on the beach and looking out to sea on a clear day. Where a ship appears on the *horizon* (or the line that is formed where the earth meets the sky) is your vanishing point. As the ship comes up around the curve of the earth, you'll see more and more of it and, of course, it will appear larger as it comes closer.

The horizon can be a smooth, semi-curved line as in looking out to sea, or it may have a rolling hills look. It might be a mountain line, or a line formed by the tops of trees. In any case, it is always *horizontal* or going in the same basic direction as the surface of the earth.

Once horizontal is understood, you must explain that *vertical* is a line going in the opposite direction. Both types of lines are very important in drawing in perspective, so be sure your students understand them. Have them show you vertical and horizontal by placing their ruler on their paper in those two directions while you check.

Now you can explain *parallel* by showing the students that when the ruler is laid horizontally on their paper, it is also parallel to the top and bottom of the paper, and when it is positioned vertically, it will be parallel to both sides of the paper. *Parallel* means "extending in the same direction and at the same distance apart at all points." It is imperative that students understand this concept because eventually, diagonal lines will be introduced on the drawing, and their eyes will have to overcome the illusion created by the perspective so that they will still be able to draw vertical or horizontal lines when necessary. Also, these diagonal lines, when connected to the v.p., will be used to draw things as they go back into the picture. They are called *converging* lines and they will "come together" at the vanishing point (v.p.).

2. Draw the horizon just above the center of the paper, with a vanishing point (v.p.) placed on the approximate center of the horizon. (See Figure 4-16.) This line is at the eye level of the viewer. (If the horizon and v.p. are moved up or down, the viewpoint changes to a worm's eye or bird's eye view. This kind of experimentation can be encouraged after students have mastered the basic skills.)

3. Using a ruler, draw the road coming from the v.p. to the picture plane (shape of the paper). Add the passing lines.

4. Draw two symbolic houses, one on each side of the road, leaving a

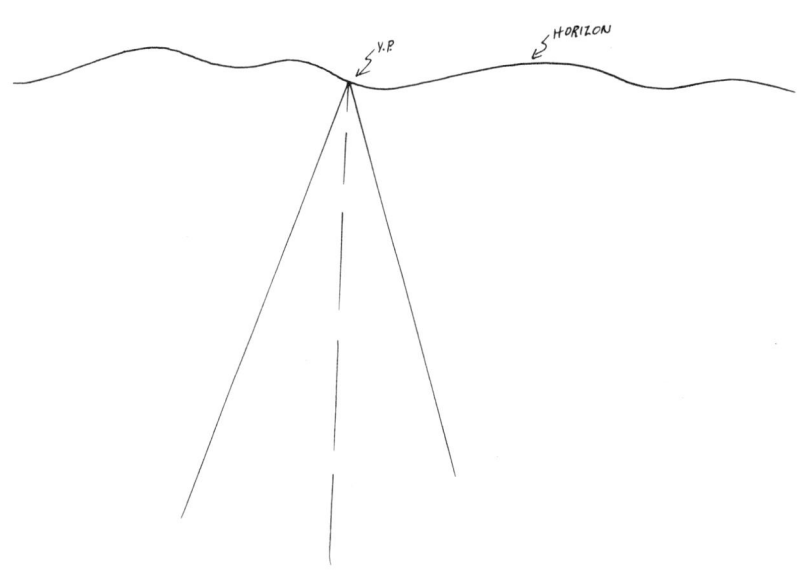

Figure 4-16

little room on the side away from the road for garages or extensions. Use the ruler properly by holding it in place with spread fingers and drawing with vertical and horizontal lines.

    5. Make the roof by putting a dot just above the center of two side lines and finishing with a ruler. Some measuring might be done here so that the height of the house will be the same on both sides. The two houses can be made a bit different in size for variety. (See Figure 4-17.)

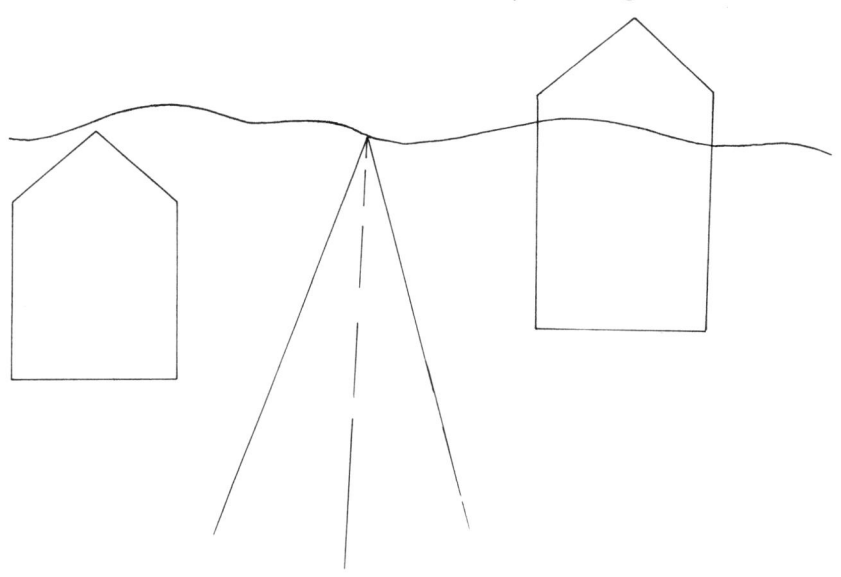

Figure 4-17

Draw out talents   **131**

    6. Draw converging lines from every corner of each house to the v.p. without drawing across the house. (See Figure 4-18.) Explain that these lines are parallel although they appear to converge—and that converging lines in perspective drawing are parallel in reality.

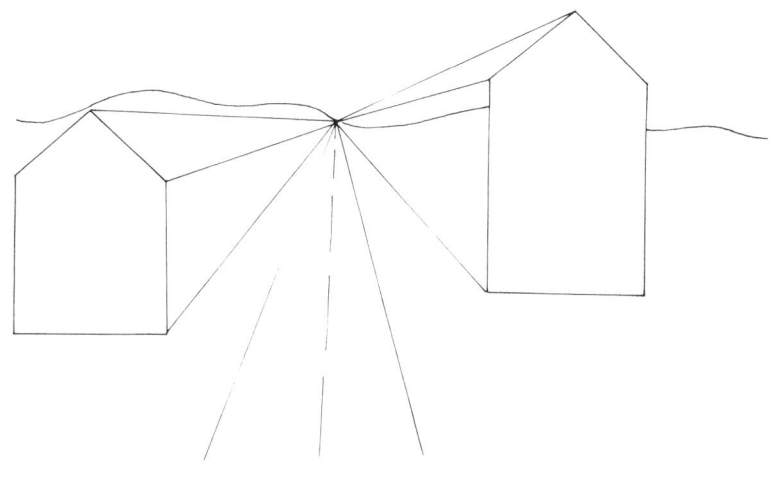

Figure 4-18

    7. Place the ruler across the entire paper, perpendicular to the top and bottom of the paper (or forming perfect T's at the top and bottom). Decide how long the houses will be and draw the back end of each house by drawing a vertical line only between the converging lines that come from the bottom and top corners of the house. Keep checking to see that the ruler is always parallel to the sides of the paper—the tendency will be to tilt the ruler because of the converging lines. (See Figure 4-19.)

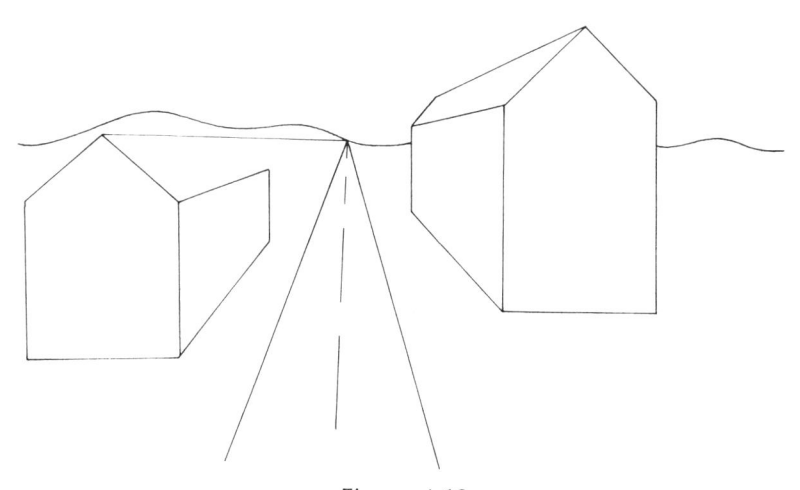

Figure 4-19

8. Erase leftover converging lines. Then connect the floating corner of the house to the roof line with a diagonal or slanted line that is parallel to the original roof line. Draw this easily by placing the ruler edge on that floating corner and matching it to the front roof edge by eye. Erase excess converging lines.

9. Make one house into a one-story home with a door and windows and draw the other with two floors, a door, windows, and an attached garage. This is made by adding a box and using v.p., vertical and horizontal lines for depth. (See Figures 4-20 and 4-21.)

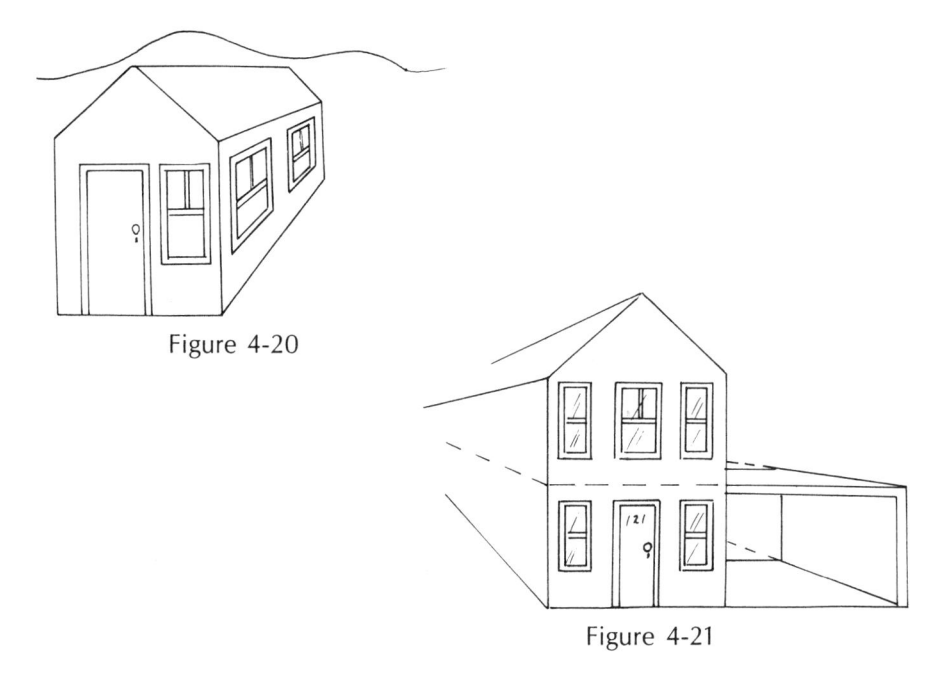

Figure 4-20

Figure 4-21

10. On both houses, drawn lines on the symbolic house shape are vertical or horizontal, but on the converging sides, the windows and doors are drawn with only vertical and converging lines.

11. Draw driveways and sidewalks, using the ruler and the v.p. Connect each bottom corner of the garage door or house door to the v.p. and extend paths or driveways out toward the viewer. Use horizontal lines to turn them toward the road and to make paths from the sides of the houses. (See Figure 4-22.)

12. Use v.p., vertical, and horizontal lines to add details—a chimney, pool, patio. (See Figure 4-23.)Telephone poles, trees, or a fence can be added by drawing two lines from the v.p. to establish location and height. Vertical lines between those guides will become poles, fence or trees.

Draw out talents 133

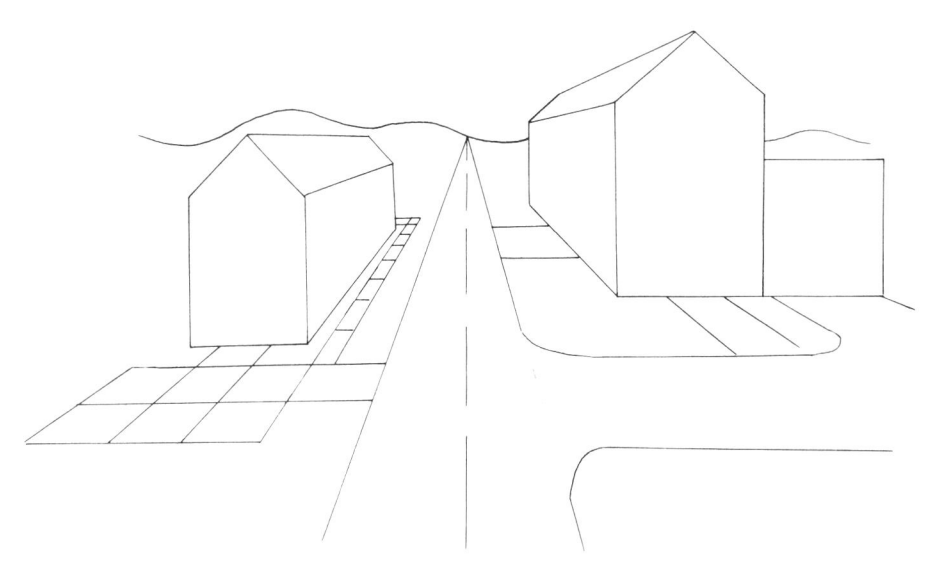

Figure 4-22

Figure 4-23

13. Add "life" to the picture—curtains, people, flowers, dog house and mailbox. Siding on the house is easy, too. Put a series of dots along the corner of the house near the road. Connect them to the v.p. and draw lines on the side. The front is finished with horizontal lines.

Variations:

The lesson can be used to draw particular scenes where the symbolic house can be changed to an office building or factory. The road could become a train track or a river. The house shape could also be a tent, with the whole scene becoming a campsite. The possibilities are endless!

Uses:

The new vocabulary can be incorporated in everyday conversation, and perspective can be used to illustrate stories, write reports, and decorate bulletin boards. Its uses never run out.

trees with U's and V's

(drawing trees)

Grade Levels: 4-6　　　　　　　　　　**Time Needed 40-80 minutes**

Before You Begin:

Next to people, trees are the most common items drawn by youngsters for fun or for academic-related illustrations. Thus, tree drawing should be established early in their drawing experiences. Ask your students to draw a tree, preferably bare, on scrap paper. In order that the drawings can be discussed wihout embarrassing anyone, they should not be signed. Display all of the drawings and discuss some of these general points with your students. (See Figure 4-24.)

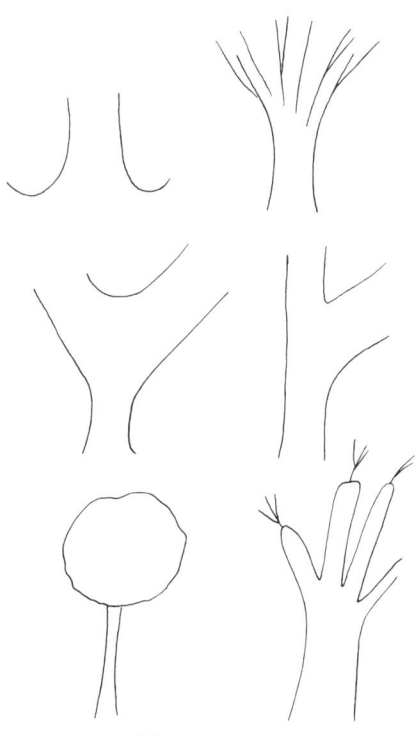

Figure 4-24

136 *Draw out talents*

- Most trees do not "swoop" out of the ground with curved trunks.
- There are no "holes" down through the tops of the trees that lead into the trunk center because all limbs and branches are connected to one another.
- Trees are the thickest at the bottom of the trunk and gradually get thinner as they go up
- Limbs are usually thinner than the place from which they grow on the trunk.
- Trees should not look like lollipops.
- Branches "branch out" into smaller and smaller twigs, eventually ending in thin twigs that will support leaves. They do not end dramatically in baseball bat shapes or flat stumps.

Discuss the varied trees that have been drawn, explaining some of the basic mistakes that have been made but being sure to praise parts of each one, too. If done with diplomacy, this can be a lot of fun, and your students will begin to point out their own trees and giggle about their errors. Explain that you will be showing them a simple method by which they can draw realistic trees, using U's and V's. The students can work step-by-step with you until they understand. Let them examine the pictures of the trees you have provided, too.

Objectives:

- To present an easy way to draw difficult subject matter.
- To develop drawing skills.
- To increase awareness and observation of surroundings.
- To develop confidence in realistic interpretation.

Materials:

- scrap paper
- 9" x 12" or 12" x 18" white vellum drawing paper
- pencils
- erasers
- magazine pictures of trees

Procedure:

1. Start with the trunk drawn near the bottom of the drawing paper, using either smooth or rough lines. Smooth lines can be used to make young trees, and rough ones can be used for older trees. Consider the

thickness of the trunk, too. Thinner trees are younger and smooth; thicker trees are usually older and rough.

2. Draw both sides of the trunk up a bit and then spread the lines away from each other. (See Figure 4-25.)

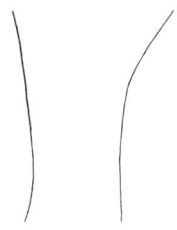

Figure 4-25

3. Form the "crotch" of the tree, the place where birds build nests, snow piles up, and squirrels sit! Apply U's or V's to begin the branches on the trunk. Show the different ways the U's and V's can be drawn. (See Figure 4-26.)

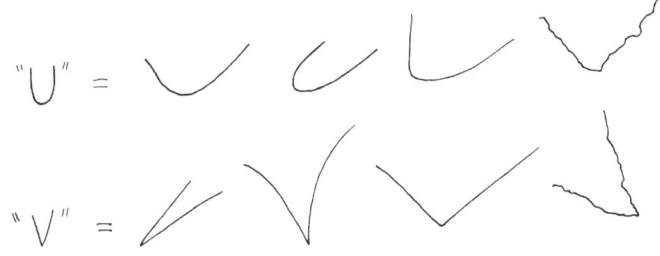

Figure 4-26

4. Do not draw these U's or V's very long. Remember that as the tree goes up, it gets thinner, so it is important to begin the branches at the precise spot where the thickness starts, or else the tree will look top-heavy. (See Figure 4-27.) Follow this procedure, making half of each U or V form two limbs with the lines on both sides.

Figure 4-27

138   *Draw out talents*

5. When the lines come too close together to separate, run them together to form the closed end of each branch with a single trailing line (or twig). Add more twigs to it. (See Figure 4-28.)

Figure 4-28

6. Look at the tree and decide if there are bare areas. If so, add another limb or small branch here and there by erasing a spot along the trunk or limb and inserting it. Then add the U's, V's and twigs. The U's will be used close to the trunk and the V's will have to be used out near the ends of branches. Remind students that leaves only grow from twigs. Have them visualize leaves on their tree and add more twigs to accommodate them where necessary.

7. Add something to the tree to enhance the drawing—a few leaves to represent the end of autumn, along with a basket and rake; an old wooden swing or tire hung from a rope or a tree house complete with ladder and "KEEP OUT!" sign. A mood might be set by showing sawed-off branches or adding people and animals.

8. Let the students compare their original drawings with the new one. The contrasts will be dramatic and a "Before and After" display will reinforce the skills learned.

Variation:

If trees are to be covered with leaves, follow only half of the procedure. A few limbs, divided up a little way with U's and V's, need only a representation of total foliage on top to become a summer tree. (See Figure 4-29.) Just add a few branches here and there peeking through holes in the foliage. This will be far more effective than a trunk topped with a ball of leaves!

Figure 4-29

Uses:

Tree drawings are a necessity in academic work and will be utilized automatically once the students are comfortable with the method. The lesson can also be used to research trees for science projects.

hearts and flowers
(Pennsylvania Dutch art)

Grade Level: 4-6 **Time Needed: 80 minutes**

Before You Begin:

Simplicity of line to create effective designs is the most exciting factor in the lesson. By demonstrating the symmetrical process as a means to develop a tree or plant with hearts, flowers, and birds springing from the branches and stems, you will make your students eager to begin their own designs. Put components of these designs on the chalkboard or provide research material that the youngsters can refer to as they begin their work.

Objectives:

- To develop a design sense in students through the employment of simple shapes and lines.
- To present an awareness of composition and a feel for its value in arrangements of shape and line.
- To demonstrate the use of symmetry to perform design.
- To introduce basic Pennsylvania Dutch art elements.
- To reinforce pleasing color choices and application through the use of crayon.

Materials:

- 18" x 24" white vellum drawing paper
- pencils
- erasers
- marking pens
- crayons
- information on Pennsylvania Dutch signs and designs

Procedure:

1. Fold the paper in half to prepare an area to draw. Depending on the fold chosen, the area to cover will either be tall and thin or short and wide.

Therefore, draw trees, tall plants, and flowers on paper with a long vertical fold, and vine-type plants or flowers on paper with a short vertical fold. (See Figure 4-30.)

Figure 4-30

2. Draw the stem or trunk along the center fold. Use light pencil drawing that can easily be erased until the sketch is satisfactory. A heart could be used as a base from which plants will grow. Fill in the spaces between branches and vines and at the ends with Pennsylvania Dutch design components: hearts (for love), the "distelfink" or bird (for good luck), and triple tulips, (for faith, hope and charity). Other designs are oak leaves, stars, daisies and clover. Much can be done with just a few of these elements. (See Figure 4-31.)

3. Remember that halves of shapes must be drawn against the fold, so if triple tulips are needed, one and one-half must be drawn. (See Figure 4-32.) Put a bird or two on the branches and add hearts, leaves, and "tear drops." Encourage filling the paper or possibly tapering the design toward the top of the folded side to form a "tree."

4. When the half-design is completed, make sure all lines are far enough apart to accommodate tracing by marking pen. Use a dark-colored marking pen to outline the design. (See Figure 4-33.) Once the

half-drawing is traced, erase any pencil marks that show. Then turn the folded half over and, using the same dark marking pen, trace the line that shows through the paper.

5. Open up the paper to complete the design. Fill in all of the areas with crayon. Coloring can match on both halves to be authentic, if desired. If it seems that there are empty areas in the completed design, fold and add more shapes in pencil to the original half of the drawing. Then continue as before.

Figure 4-31

Figure 4-32

Figure 4-33

Variations:

The paper could be cut into large circles, folded, and designed as a more typical Pennsylvania Dutch hex sign. Smaller circles could be used for the designs and, when completed, mounted on a "barn door" background, a typical sight in the Pennsylvania Dutch area.

Uses:

The history of the Pennsylvania Dutch settlers, and the meanings of the various designs used in their art, form an interesting area of study to tie in with this lesson.

5

Everyone's an artist!

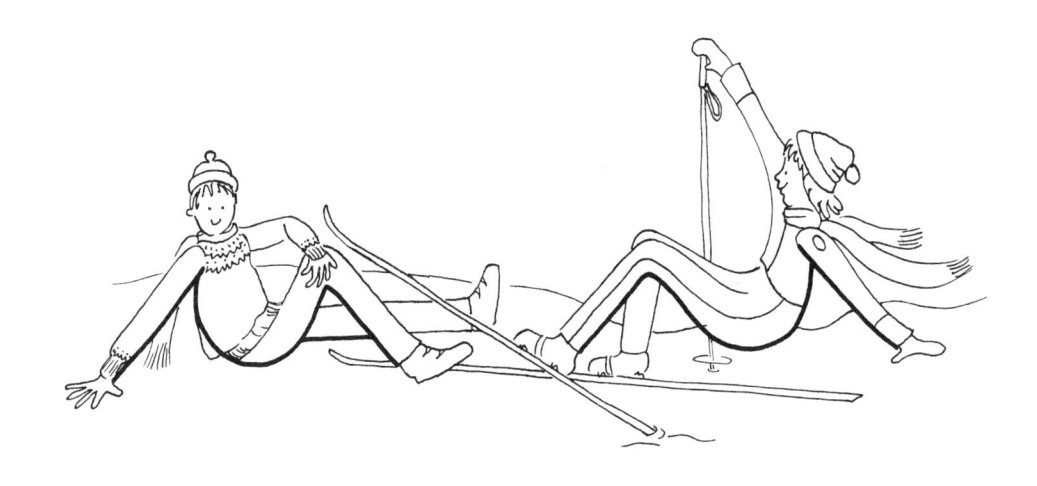

These lessons are unique drawing experiences that will familiarize your students with new dimensions in drawing and also develop their drawing skills. Emphasis is placed on humor because, although the fourth, fifth, and sixth graders know what is funny, they often are unable to express it effectively. Thus, these lessons provide a background for humor that will come naturally as a result of media exposure and everyday life experiences.

starting with something
(elaborating upon a line drawing)

Grade Levels: 4-6   **Time Needed: 40-80 minutes**

Before You Begin:

Elaborate upon a few sketches you will provide as a stimulus for this lesson. Encourage your students to go "a little crazy" with their own drawings, getting different ideas by turning the sketch upside down or sideways.

Objectives:

- To provide a different approach to drawing.
- To create unusual drawings through thinking and planning.
- To develop self-confidence in drawing.

Materials:

- 9" x 12" drawing paper
- 12" x 18" drawing paper
- 18" x 24" drawing paper
- a copy of a drawing for each student, preferably a line drawing from a newspaper or magazine (see Figures 5-1 and 5-2)
- pencils
- erasers
- scissors
- paste
- drawing ink and pens (optional)
- colored pencils, markers, watercolors

Procedure:

1. Give each student a copy of the stimulant sketch. Examine and turn the drawing around until an idea develops.
2. Mount the sketch on drawing paper. The size of the drawing paper depends on what will be done to elaborate the sketch. Placement of the sketch is important, so plan this before mounting it.

Figure 5-1

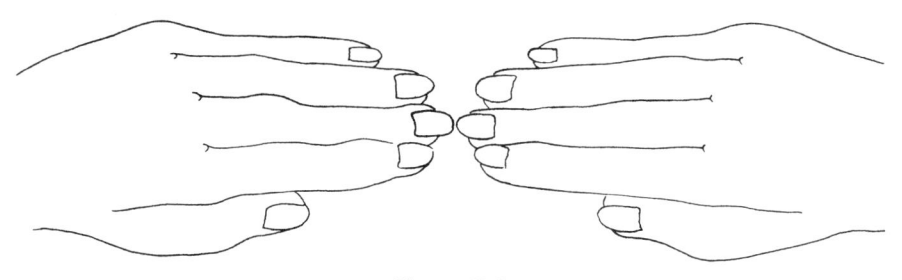

Figure 5-2

3. Add details, such as background and surrounding items, to the object or character—the more, the better. Blend together the original sketch (see Figure 5-3) and the additions so that the observer cannot tell where one stops and the other begins. (See Figures 5-4 and 5-5.) Perhaps ink could be used if the original drawing resembles an ink drawing. Otherwise, blend pencil, colored pencils, markers or watercolors on both the original and the drawn parts of the picture.

Figure 5-3

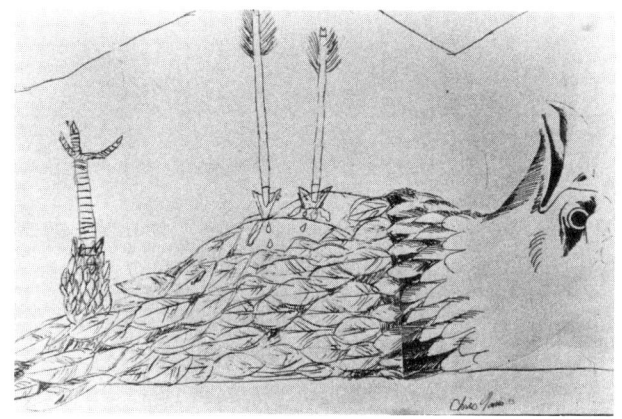

Figure 5-4

Figure 5-5

Uses:

Use this lesson to research other people and their native dress, surroundings, and habits by providing a head to be researched and completed. Scientific study of the human systems might also be done with this lesson, with younger children filling in a body outline with the nervous system, digestive system, respiratory system, etc.

Creative writing is a natural outgrowth of this type of drawing process. Encourage your students to develop short stories, poems, or sayings to accompany their drawings.

148 Everyone's an artist

rough and tumble
(winter action figures)

Grade Levels: 4-6 **Time Needed: 80 minutes**

Before You Begin:

Demonstrate drawing people from the six formulas for the students. They will be ready to draw these figures when they see how easy it is to make fully dressed, real-looking people with little effort.

Objectives:

- To draw people simply and effectively.
- To achieve more realistic poses and eliminate the habit of always drawing people from the front and in the same position.
- To gain confidence in drawing the human figure from memory.
- To learn new vocabulary: background and foreground.

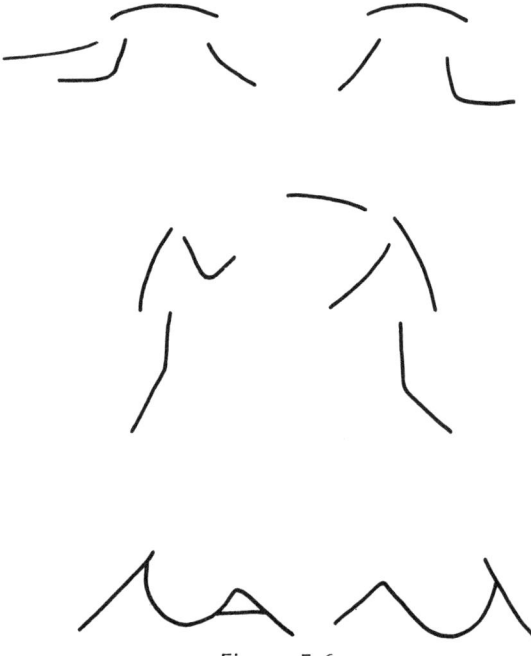

Figure 5-6

Materials:

- 9" x 12" drawing paper
- 18" x 24" drawing paper
- pencils
- erasers
- colored pencils or marking pens
- the six formulas displayed on chart paper

Procedure:

1. Look at the six formulas for body drawing (see Figure 5-6) and copy each one as you begin to draw the people.

2. Practice making people using all six formulas, and repeating some with variations. (See Figures 5-7, 5-8, and 5-9.) Use the smaller paper and draw two figures on a sheet. These people can be colored with markers or colored pencils.

3. Make a snow scene on the larger paper, using all of the formulas and repeating some to fill the picture. (See Figure 5-10.) Remember to make larger people in the foreground and smaller ones in the background.

Figure 5-7

Figure 5-8

150   *Everyone's an artist*

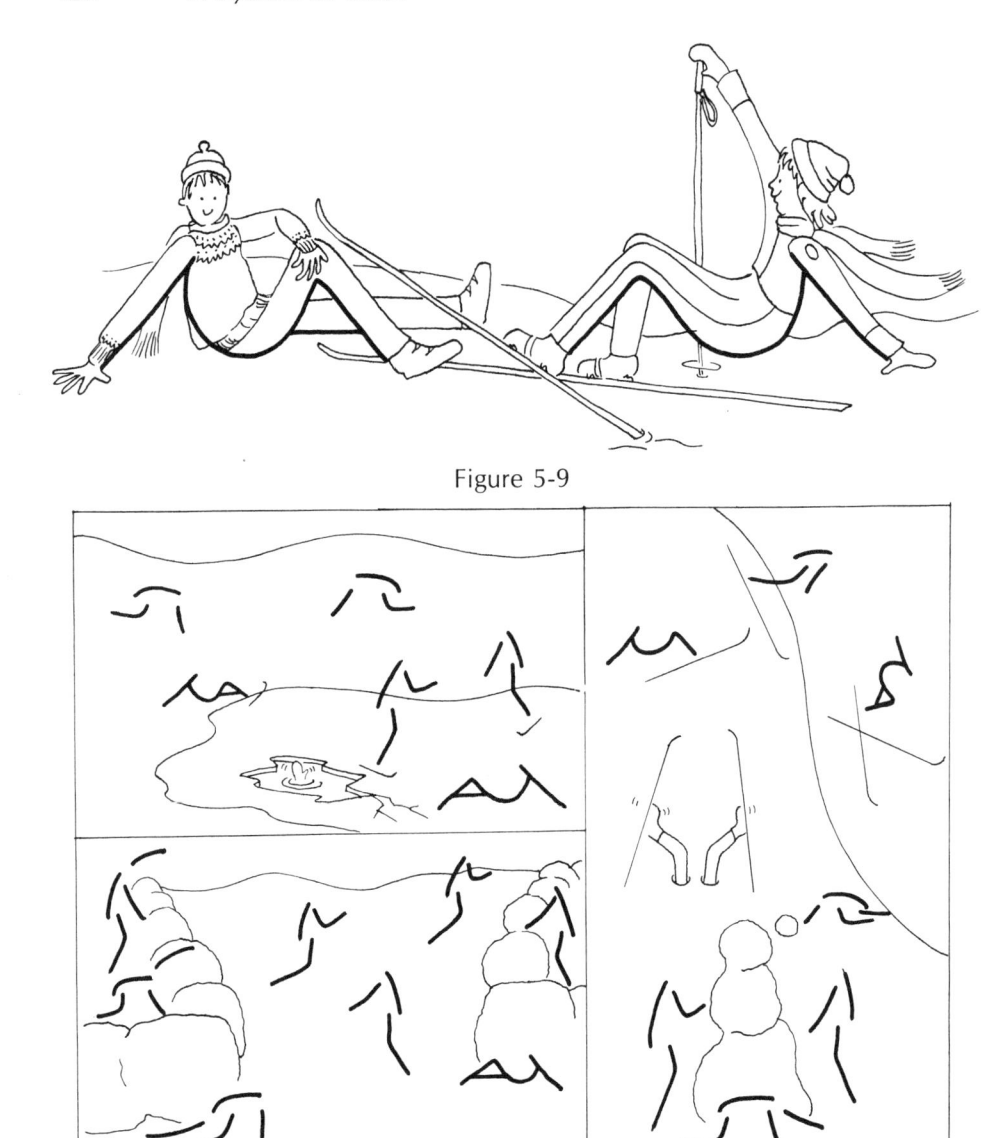

Figure 5-9

Figure 5-10

4. Add simple sketches of skis, skates, sleds, snowballs being thrown, snowmen, cracks and holes in ice, an edge of a pond, ski jumps, and distant hills for small figures. (See Figure 5-11.)

5. Complete the scene so that it becomes a skating party, teams of children in snow forts throwing snowballs, building snowmen, a skiing scene, or sleds and toboggans zipping down hills. NOTE: Discourage the inclusion of sky in the background. If the whole paper is considered "snow" or "ice," there will be more room for figure drawing.

Figure 5-11

6. Color the scene with colored pencils and fine-tip markers. Snow can be shadowed here and there with light blue.

Variation:

These figures can be used for mural work with each student choosing his or her own formula and positions to complete a large scene. Some students could sketch in the background—hills, ski jumps, a pond or lake, and the beginning of a snow fort. Other students could then go to the background mural at various times during the day and add their own figures.

Uses:

Use the formulas for people in athletic clothes for sport performances. Just add the proper clothing for the sport desired and draw scenes depicting the sport.

The possibilities are endless, and can carry over into other academic areas, such as story illustrations and creative writing.

___ that's my name, want my address? ___
(letter and name designs)

Grade Levels: 4-6　　　　　　　　　**Time Needed: 80 minutes**

Before You Begin:

Show a few examples of designs composed of names made up of capital and lower case, script and print. They may be done exclusively in pen or markers, or a combination of both. The finished name can assume any shape, such as a heart, square, rectangle, triangle, or circle. Unusual shapes like a shield, a flower, or a boat can also be developed by lightly sketching the final contour in pencil and filling in the letters against the pencil line.

Objectives:

- To provide an awareness of various lettering techniques.
- To develop consistency and control in performance.
- To experiment with design and composition, using common elements.

Materials:

- 9" x 12" white vellum drawing paper
- marking pens
- ballpoint pens
- colored pencils
- rulers
- examples of different types of letters cut out from magazines and newspapers
- opaque projector (optionaal)
- 18" x 24" or 24" x 36" drawing paper (optional)

Procedure:

1. Begin with the first letter of the first name. Make it simple or elaborate, plain or decorated, flat or three dimensional in appearance.

Add the rest of the name around this central letter, one letter at a time, and repeat it to form the design. (See Figure 5-12.) If duplicate letters are together, have the first one in script and the second one in print to show the difference. Middle names may be used, but if the design will be too cumbersome, just use the middle initial, then the last name.

Figure 5-12

2. Consistency should be emphasized, and letters may be normal handwriting size or miniature.

3. Color in areas, fill in letters, and outline or double certain letters to complete the design.

4. Mount the finished design on contrasting paper and display on a bulletin board or use as a border.

Variation:

When the designs are completed, illuminate and enlarge them on a wall by using the opaque projector. Use either 18" x 24" or 24" x 36" paper on which to reproduce the designs. Notice that the simple lines made in pen or marker now have thickness and have to be reproduced as double lines. Use a ruler to help trace some letters, then color. These posters will be colorful room decorations.

Uses:

The names could be changed to protect the innocent! Have students choose the name of a real personality, such as a politician, movie star, sports figure, or a fantasy or cartoon character. The letter designs can be decorated according to the character. For example, the President's name could be done in red, white and blue, with stars and stripes; Superman's design should start out with the appropriate "S"; and an "Alice in Wonderland" theme could be decorated with teacups, rabbit ears, and hearts. (See Figure 5-13.) Use these designs to decorate the empty areas of your classroom.

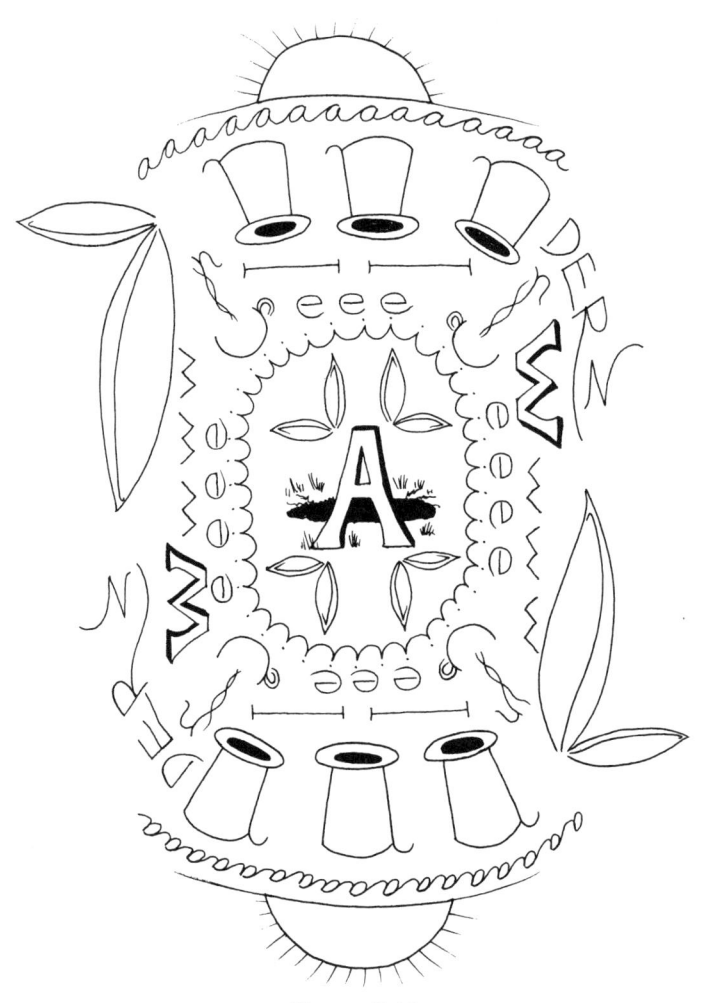

Figure 5-13

using your thumb
(symmetrical object drawing)

Grade Levels: 5-6   **Time Needed: 40-120 minutes**

Before You Begin:

Demonstrate this technique to show the ease by which visible objects can be reproduced. You might stimulate interest by drawing flowers in a bottle, or a mouse peeping from behind a pot.

Objectives:

- To provide the opportunity for intense observation.
- To learn the technique of measuring proportion in the air with a stick, a thumb, and one's eye.
- To develop the awareness of symmetry and learn how to record it.
- To gain confidence in drawing correctly.
- To learn and use new vocabulary: setup, axis, contour, ellipse, symmetrical, asymmetrical, horizontal, and vertical.

Materials:

- 12" x 18" drawing paper
- pencils
- rulers
- colored pencils
- measuring sticks (12-inch dowels, unsharpened pencils, paint brushes)
- sandpaper
- symmetrical objects to use as models

Procedure:

1. Make a setup of a few objects in the center of the work area. Be sure the students sit close enough to the objects to get a good-sized drawing when each measurement is doubled.

2. Lightly draw an axis line down the center of the paper or wherever the center of the object will be located.

3. Remember these important points: Do not move once the measuring and drawing have started; use sandpaper for sharpening pencils. Always take measurements from the same point in space, so lock the measuring elbow every time; hold the stick perpendicular every time; and always measure with the upper torso against the back of the chair.

4. Following these points, close one eye and hold the measuring stick in the drawing hand.

5. Measure top to bottom of the object by placing the sticktip in line with the top of the object and the thumbnail at the bottom, sliding it up and down until on target. Record this measurement twice by marking a pencil dot with the other hand at the top of the axis, and then at the thumbnail position. Move the sticktip down to the thumbnail marking and mark *again* at the thumbnail. The vertical measurement is now in proportion and doubled.

6. Take and record horizontal (width) measurements the same way, with one measurement being recorded on each side of the axis. Take a measurement with the ruler to test for accuracy from the axis. If the object has sections that are of different widths, take several measurements and record on both sides of the axis.

7. Fill in the shapes by looking at the outline of the object (contour), and following the pencil dots.

8. Some things to look for when drawing bottles, cups, pots, jars, and cans: ellipses ("squashed" circles) are created by looking at round objects from the side. This means that a partial ellipse is seen at the bottom of the object and a whole ellipse is seen at the top, as in an open can, for example. (See Figure 5-14.) NOTE: The ellipse goes up from the bottom on both sides of the axis, and down at the top. (See Figure 5-15.) Also, the ellipse should not have any points because it is still a circle, no matter in which way it is seen. (See Figure 5-16.)

Figure 5-14

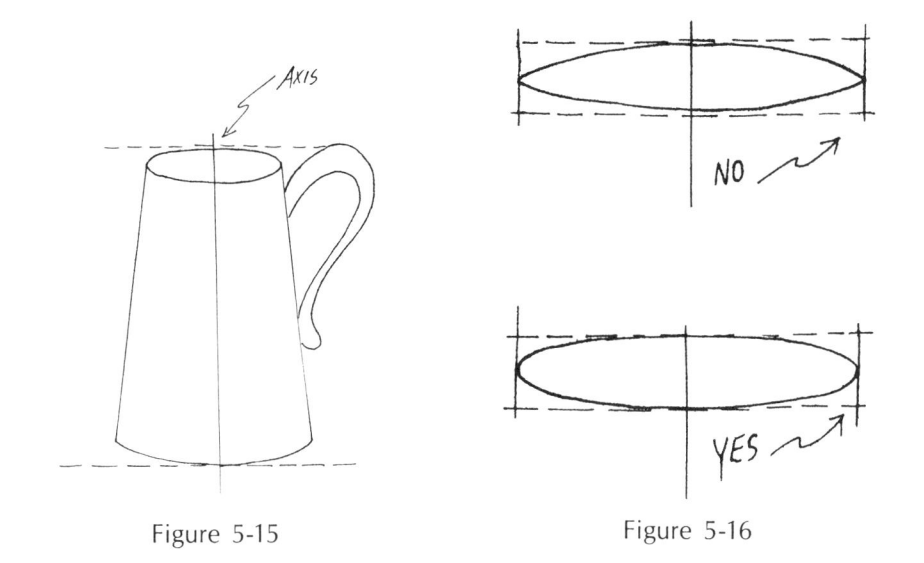

Everyone's an artist 157

Figure 5-15

Figure 5-16

9. Add an asymmetrical section to the object, like an open lid, handle, or spout. Measure down the axis and over, by eye, to establish where connections occur. (See Figure 5-17.)

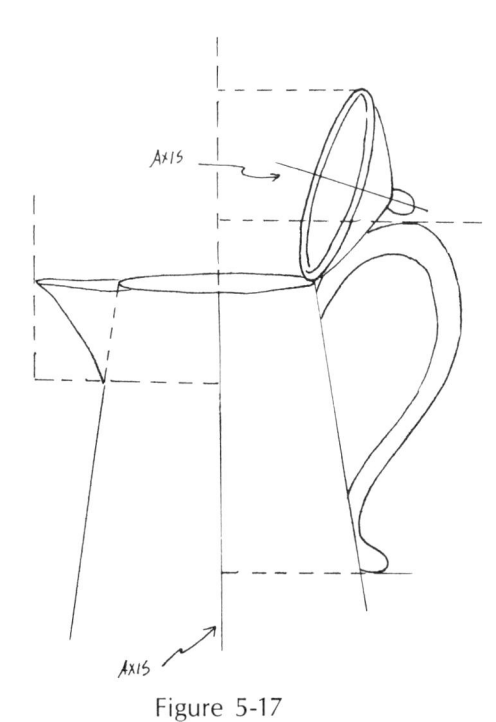

Figure 5-17

10. More objects may be added by establishing another axis for each one.

11. Decorate bottles and pots with labels and designs. Use colored pencils to enhance the finished drawing.

Variations:

This technique can be used to draw larger objects, such as a chair, a bicycle, and people. The use of more than one object from different locations, combined to form odd combinations, is an interesting variation for older students. These drawings can then be filled with paint, pastels, or markers.

I gotta hand it to ya
(contour drawing — cartoons)

Grade Levels: 5-6   **Time Needed: 80-120 minutes**

Before You Begin:

You should practice this lesson several times before trying it with your students. Then your examples with cartoon additions can be shown to the children so that they understand what is expected. In addition, let them watch closely as you demonstrate the method. The cartoon aspect of the drawing will appeal to the students. They will be eager to position their models (hands and shoes) in unusual fashions to accommodate some of the crazy ideas they will think of for the final drawing.

Objectives:

- To learn a new method of drawing.
- To realize a dramatic improvement in drawing results.
- To recognize prominent line features by using a contour.
- To stress the importance of observation in being able to draw.
- To develop drawing skills.
- To increase concentration potential.
- To develop a sense of humor.
- To become aware of the use of common objects in art.
- To produce unique drawings that demonstrate the contour techniques.

Materials:

- 12" x 18" newsprint paper
- 12" x 18" white vellum drawing paper
- ballpoint pens
- pens
- students' hands and (unusual) shoes
- *The Natural Way to Draw,* by Kimon Nicolaides

Procedure:

1. Explain that "contour" means outline, and that students must practice seeing the model as a flat picture rather than as a three-dimensional form. They will transfer what they see to the pencil by concentration.

2. Before starting, remember these important points about contour drawing: do *not* look at the paper; start to draw at one point and end at the same point; slowly move the eyes along the outline or contour of the object as though the eyes are scissors, cutting the object out of the space around it; move the pencil along the paper very slowly, drawing *exactly* the contour that the eyes are following; and use total concentration. Remind the students of these points as they draw. NOTE: A good resource that explains this method is *The Natural Way to Draw: A Working Plan for Art Study* by Kimon Nicolaides (Boston: Houghton Mifflin, copyright 1941 by Anne Nicolaides).

3. Place the non-drawing hand in a comfortable position on the paper. NOTE: Use newsprint paper until the technique is mastered, then white vellum for final attempts.

4. Look at the wrist and place the pen on the paper; then begin.

5. Moving the eyes and pen at the same rate of speed, "cut out" the hand from the space around it, sticking to the outside outline of the hand. Students must constantly remind their pen to wait for, or catch up to, their eye. This comes more easily after several tries. Come back around to the bottom of the wrist. (See Figure 5-18.) This will not be a closed contour

Figure 5-18   Figure 5-19

unless there is a sleeve or cuff edge, or perhaps a watch that can be drawn to complete the contour.

6. Do not move the modeling hand after the contour is complete. All of the clues along the outside contour—the lumps and bumps—help to establish the interior drawing of the hand. Now use all of the nooks and crannies on the outline to locate and draw the interior sections. Glance down occasionally at the modeling hand, but the drawing should still be done slowly and in a constant movement rather than a "sketchy" one. (See Figure 5-19.)

7. Once the hand has been completed, draw in the contour additions. (See Figure 5-20.)

Figure 5-20

8. Use the same technique with a shoe as the model. (See Figure 5-21.) Try shoes of different sizes and styles. Finished cartoons may depict fantasy or realism.

162   *Everyone's an artist*

Figure 5-21

Variations:

This technique can be used to draw any object or combination of objects. Also, models might pose in a central location for students to try "contour people." Any attempt at contour drawing will develop the drawing skills of the students, so the lesson should be repeated several times, with different objects as models.

The technique is also very useful for copy work that your students often do in correlation with academic areas. Map and animal illustrations are much more effective if contour drawing is used to copy from reference books. Straight copies usually tend to be small, with the eraser used more often than the pencil! But with contour drawing, the results will be larger, more fluid and recognizable.

mug shots
(profiles and frontals)

Grade Level: 6 **Time Needed: 80 minutes**

Before You Begin:

Children love to draw funny faces, and profiles are the easiest to draw because students can go wild with funny noses, jutting chins, and big eyes. Let the students do comic and cartoon research by keeping a cartoon file made up of clips from newspapers and comic books. When a collecion of samples has been built up, demonstrate the procedure for the students. Then watch them create!

Objectives:

- To use different methods and techniques for making profiles and frontals; estimating and measuring.
- To become more confident in drawing by using a ruler.
- To learn new vocabulary: profile, axis.

Materials:

- 12" x 18" white drawing paper
- pencils
- erasers
- rulers
- colored pencils (optional)

Procedure:

1. Fold the paper in half and begin a profile by making the nose first. Make it close to the fold, facing the empty half of the paper, and work large enough so that the completed head will more or less fill the half of the paper. NOTE: Here is a trick for making a good profile: draw a light slanted line with a ruler from the nose down. (See Figure 5-22.) No matter what kind of lips and chins are drawn, use this guide and draw behind it. A "pretty" face can be achieved by strictly using the guide, while a funny

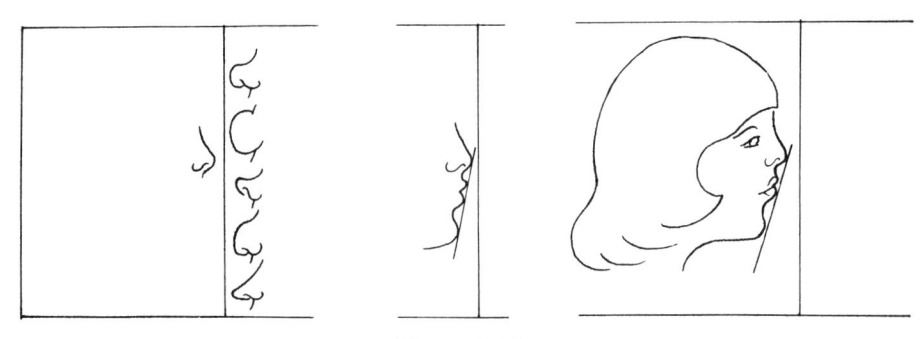

Figure 5-22

face can be drawn by surpassing the guide with a jutting chin or large mouth.

2. When the profile, back of head, and hair are completed, put in the nostril, eye (side view), eyebrow, lashes, ear, and any other details, such as freckles, warts, glasses, eyepatch, bandage, scars, beard, jewelry, hat, or hair ornament. (See Figure 5-23.)

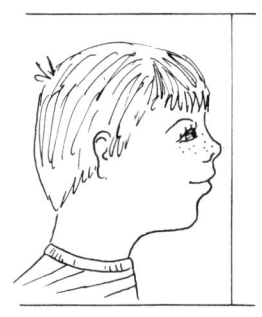

Figure 5-23

3. To make the frontal extension, unfold the paper and start with an axis (middle-of-the-face line) in light pencil with the ruler, down through the center of the empty half of the paper. Using the ruler horizontally, extend all details of the face from the original profile and mark in their positions along the axis.

4. Start with the top of the head or hat and the bottom of the chin. Those features outside the axis must be marked: eyes, nose, nostrils, eyebrows, cheeks, cheekbones, mouth, etc. Some of these marks must be estimated, but use the axis at all times to measure evenly, as in the location and size of the eyes.

5. The width of the face may be established first or last, but fit the features in the outside shape in such a manner as to develop the character's face. (See Figure 5-24.) For example, a fat face may have tiny features, and a thin, long face may have oversized features. The final effect

Everyone's an artist 165

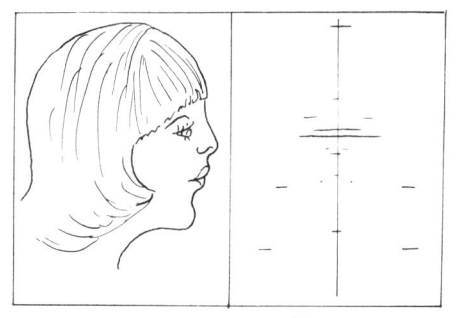

Figure 5-24

to be developed is that of a "mug shot," a face that has turned from a side position to a front view.

6. As the frontal view is being developed, take care to work back and forth between the two sketches to maintain the same "value" (darkness and lightness) in drawing, shading, and details. (See Figure 5-25.)

Figure 5-25

7. Be sure, also, to extend the neck down from right under the ears. (See Figure 5-26.) This eliminates a "head on a pole" look.

8. Complete the drawing by cleaning up all guidelines and horizontal markings. Colored pencils may be used to give the drawings a more lifelike look. Black and white sketches may be elaborated to resemble "wanted" signs.

Variations:

Students may do a series of cartoons... a family with similar characteristics, several clowns or other characters.

Although size should not be varied, subject matter can be. Students might want to design whole characters, animal faces, and objects, such as two views of a chair, teapot, banana split, or car.

166   *Everyone's an artist*

Figure 5-26

Everyone's an artist 167

— *you take one half, I'll take the other* —
(complete a face)

Grade Level: 6   **Time Needed: 80 minutes**

Before You Begin:

Save yourself some preparation time by displaying the examples shown in Figure 5-27. All of these examples were completed by sixth-graders. On seeing the finished pictures, your students will understand what is expected of them, but you will still have to explain how to go about setting up the face. Provide plenty of faces for the students to choose from and you will soon see some exciting drawings.

Figure 5-27

Objectives:

- To understand and demonstrate the meaning of "value."
- To experiment with copy work.
- To practice drawing facial features.
- To encourage expanded thinking and free-hand realistic drawing.

Materials:

- a black-and-white magazine face for each student. (NOTE: Cut the picture in half exactly through the middle. Use only one half of each face in a particular class; save the other halves for a different class. Minimum size should be two inches.)
- 9" x 12" white vellum drawing paper
- 2B drawing pencils
- erasers
- rulers
- paste

Procedure:

1. Choose a face half and trim away any excess paper, if it is marred by advertisement. Otherwise, keep the rectangular format.
2. Paste the face half to the drawing paper, leaving enough space in the appropriate places for the extended drawings. Rings of clear tape on the back can also be used, for cleaner results.
3. Use a ruler to measure how far away from the center the eye should be, or how wide the head or mouth should be. Remember to work constantly in reverse of what is seen. (See Figure 5-28.)
4. When the sketch of the face is completed, try to bring up the black, grays, and whites (value) to match the original half. Color in the black first, then shade in the grays, and end with the whites. Some erasing may have to be done to get highlights.
5. Extend the picture by adding a body or completing parts of the body or objects that show. The rest of the rectangle around the face can be drawn to resemble a photo in a newspaper, or a photograph album, or a face in a window. Trimmed faces will need background details.

Uses:

This lesson might be used to develop and demonstrate studies of particular occupations. By requiring a descriptive drawing of the body in a

Everyone's an artist 169

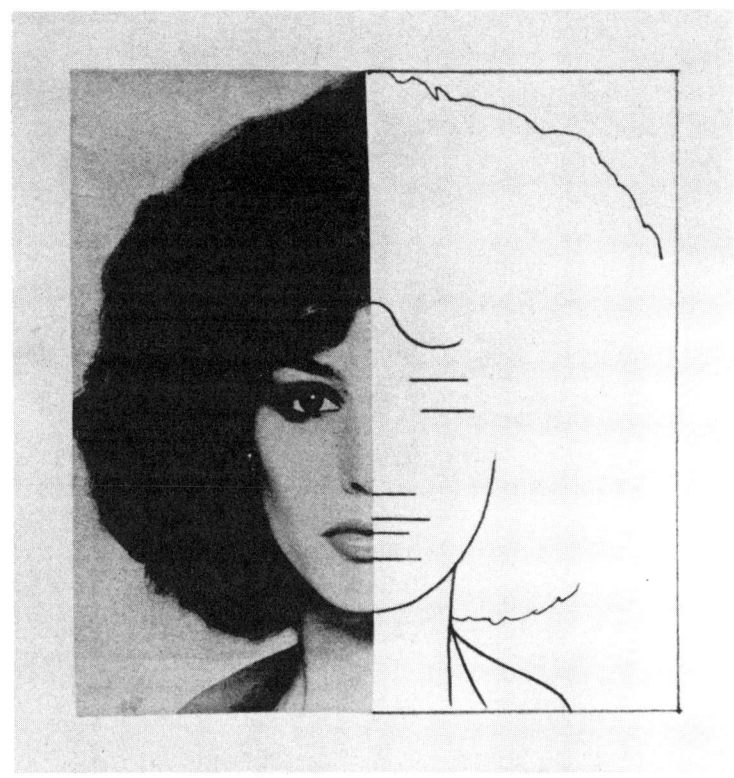

Figure 5-28

proper attire or uniform and with tools of the trade, you can ensure the portrayal of various occupations. You might also assign students to research a particular trade and develop the necessary information to identify it, starting with the person's face.

170   *Everyone's an artist*

buildings in depth
(two-point perspective)

Grade Level: 6   **Time Needed: 120-160 minutes**

Before You Begin:

Review one-point perspective (see Chapter 4's "Getting into Things") with the students and explain the vocabulary. They may want to draw a simple building in one-point perspective in order to refresh the use of the vocabulary and ruler. The realism of drawing in perspective or "going into the picture" is enough to get the students ready to perform. Explain that the plans for all of your examples are available for them to use to start a second drawing after they have mastered the concept of drawing in two-point perspective. (See Figure 5-29.) Have several starter drawings for each type

Figure 5-29

of building so the students can choose which plan they would like to follow. These plans include a castle, beach house, skyscraper, museum or theater, and an "Old West" saloon. Any of these plans can be extended or changed into another type of building; this depends on the individual students and their interests. Just give them some suggestions. For instance, the beach house plan can become a restaurant or a bait shop on a pier, the museum can be used as a factory or airport terminal, the skyscraper can be a rocket hangar, and the saloon can be turned into any kind of shop, store, or home. Let the students use their imaginations.

Objectives:

- To further understand perspective and how to achieve it.
- To reinforce perspective vocabulary.
- To develop drawing skills and the use of the ruler.
- To encourage imagination and creative use of simple plans.

Materials:

- 12" x 18" white vellum drawing paper
- 18" x 24" white vellum drawing paper
- pencils
- erasers
- rulers
- yardsticks or long straightedges
- building plans

Procedure:

1. Work through the house drawing part of the lesson until it is thoroughly understood.

2. Start two-point perspective by drawing a five-inch vertical line in the center of the paper that is closer to the bottom than the top of the paper. This is the "station point" or closest corner of the house to the viewer. Place two vanishing points (v.p.'s) at the edges of the paper that are at eye level and on an imaginary horizon line, roughly in the middle of the paper. The horizon can be put in after the drawing is completed. Using a ruler, draw from the top and bottom of the line to both v.p.'s. (See Figure 5-30.)

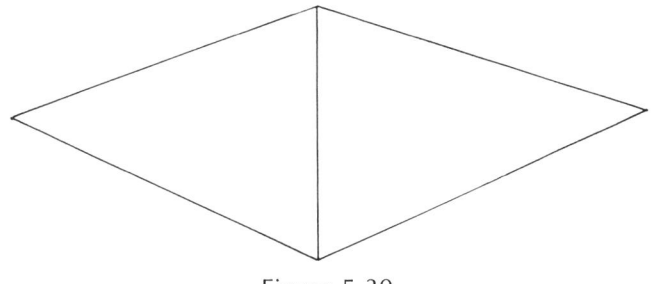

Figure 5-30

172   *Everyone's an artist*

3. Look at the drawing carefully and notice two sides of a box that disappear into the distance. These sides need to be cut off in space, a comfortable distance away from the corner, so establish two vertical lines and erase the leftover converging lines back to the v.p. (See Figure 5-31.)

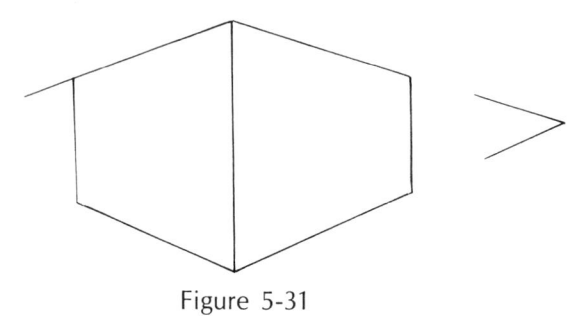

Figure 5-31

4. To find the centers of the sides of the house, draw X's from the corners of the "in perspective" rectangles. These centers can be used to establish upstairs and downstairs by using the v.p.'s to draw a line across each side of the house through the centers of the X's. The two lines should meet on the station point line, if the drawing is being done accurately. (See Figure 5-32.)

5. To raise a roof, use one of the center X's to draw a vertical line up above the house. At a comfortable angle, draw from a point on that vertical down to the two top corners of the house. (See Figure 5-32 again.) Just connect the tip of the roof to the opposite v.p. and finish with a matching diagonal roof line. This completes the house. Erase the X's and the vertical and converging line to the v.p., but keep the middle floor line until windows and doors are established.

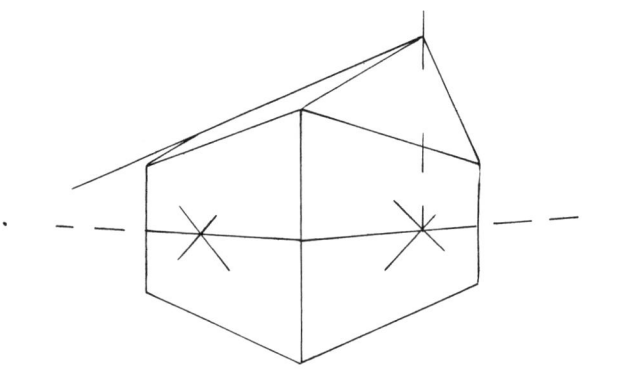

Figure 5-32

6. Lightly sketch where doors and windows will be, then use the ruler and draw all lines either vertical or toward the v.p.'s. Keep in mind the fact that this may be difficult because of the optical illusion created by the

converging lines that run back to the v.p.'s. The *depth* of the picture may create some problems in drawing vertical lines. Just remember that vertical lines are *parallel* to the side edges of the paper and *perpendicular* to the top and bottom of the paper. There are no horizontal lines in this drawing, only vertical or v.p. lines.

7. Use the ruler to draw the same-sized windows upstairs and downstairs. The half of the house closer to the v.p. will have smaller windows than the other half, although the windows would be the same size on an actual house. Use the X to establish a door in the middle of the house, if desired.

8. Paths that come out of doorways or go around the house, or roads that go past the house, are established with the v.p.'s. Use the opposite v.p. to draw out from each side of the house, but use the corresponding v.p. to draw along the sides of the house. (See Figure 5-33.)

Figure 5-33

9. If steps are desired, draw them in, then make a foundation on the house. Draw two opposite v.p. lines out from the bottom of the door, a corresponding v.p. line connecting those two lines, two vertical lines down from those corners, and another corresponding v.p. line connecting those two lines together. Start the pattern all over again and continue until the desired number of steps is completed. (See Figure 5-34.) Extend the station point line down and add a foundation to accommodate the steps.

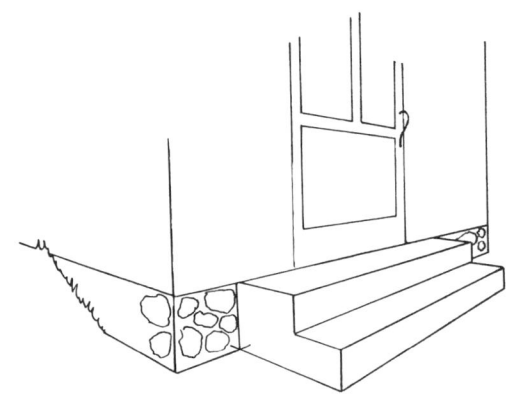

Figure 5-34

10. The basic drawing procedure is now complete, and freehand details can be added to the picture.

11. Here are five plans for extending the basic house pattern; discuss each one and show examples and plans for the students' selection. Locate the station point off center to leave room for extensions or another building. Use the larger paper and longer straightedges or yardsticks. Students may want to bring research pictures to this phase of the lesson, and you should provide magazines or brochures showing various types of buildings and homes.

Castle

Start with low v.p.'s in order to show height on the castle. A taller fairy tale castle can be drawn by turning the paper the long way and making lots of towers. The castle can also be built in a wedding-cake style by adding one station point after another, a little to one side. Add the moat by beginning a road, but then extending the castle's sides down through those lines to show depth. (See Figure 5-35.)

Beach House

This is primarily the same drawing as the basic house except that the station point is moved to the side. Add a pier by using the v.p.'s to establish a flat form under the building. (See Figure 5-36.) This may become a restaurant, fishing pier, or yacht club by adding diners entering the building, fishermen on the dock, or boats in the water!

Skyscraper

Place the v.p.'s low to give height to the building. (See Figure 5-37.) A whole block of buildings might be added by using one v.p. A sidewalk,

Everyone's an artist   175

Figure 5-35

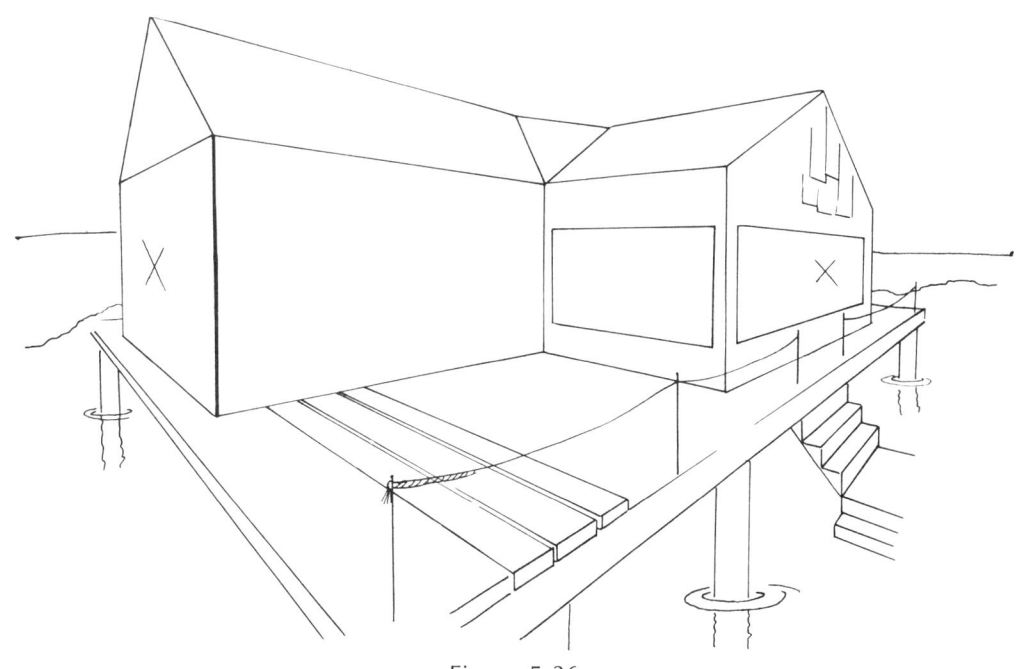

Figure 5-36

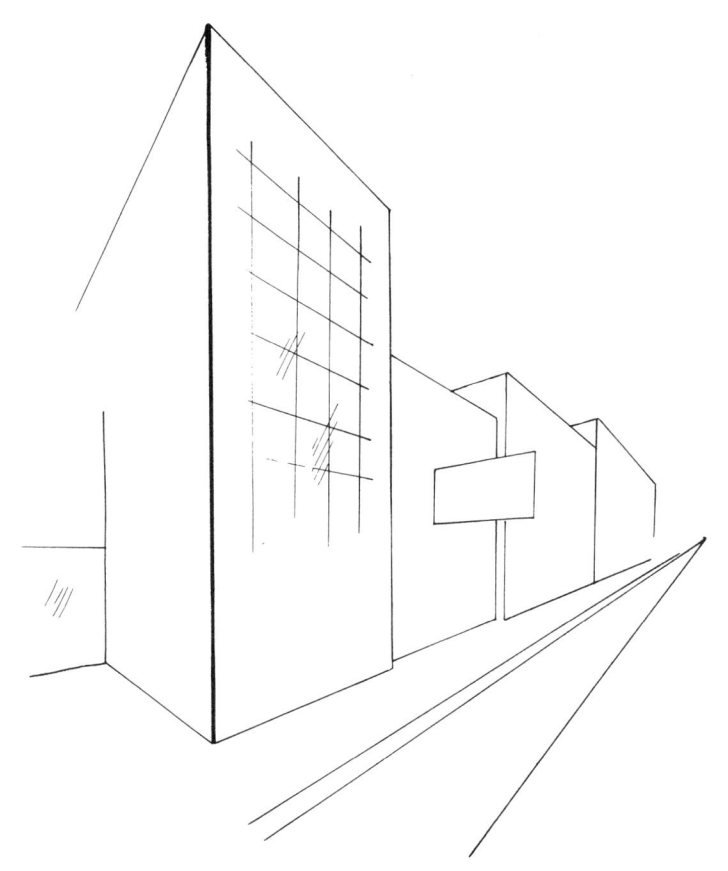

Figure 5-37

curb, and street add to authenticity, along with signs, display windows, and fire escapes.

Museum or Theater

This plan lends itself to many types of buildings, including a factory, health spa, tennis club, restaurant, or store. The steps can lead to an attractive museum or theater, but could also lead into a pool or onto a patio. Obviously, the same plan can be used to make a tall building with a courtyard or skating rink at the base if the paper is held the long way. (See Figure 5-38.)

Old West Saloon

Draw the saloon off-center to make room for a jail, bank, livery stable, or blacksmith's shop. Use an X to find the center of the facade and

Everyone's an artist 177

Figure 5-38

make the decorative shape. (See Figure 5-39.) Don't forget the "bad guys" in the back alley!

Figure 5-39

After experiencing this lesson, students should be aware of two-point perspective in everyday life. They should be encouraged to use perspective drawing on their own after drawing the house and designing a building from the plans. (See Figure 5-40.)

Figure 5-40

Uses:

The possibilities for using two-point perspective are endless. Basically, the lesson can be tied into math with the use of the ruler or meter stick for measuring. In addition, the building designs can be directed toward a particular theme—space, history, industry, architecture, etc.

6

Crafts made with unusual materials

Crafts can be quite boring, especially to children who have already done them at camp or at a summer recreation program! The lessons in this chapter, however, will keep the students totally absorbed. They are almost exclusively constructed from "junk" and introduce your students to many new skills and different finished products.

180   Try unusual materials

——— *don't shake my hand...it bites!* ———
(puppet on a hand)

Grade Levels: K-2   **Time Needed: 40 minutes**

Before You Begin:

Make one of these puppets on your hand to interest the students. The children will not need much motivation to get started on this puppet once they see how easy it is to make and how simple to operate.

Objectives:

- To create a simple puppet using few materials.
- To present an opportunity for expression by using a part of the body.
- To learn how to make simple features and props for expression.

Materials:

- non-toxic magic markers
- scraps of white paper
- yarn
- cloth scraps
- masking tape
- paste
- lightweight cardboard

Procedure:

1. Place the non-writing hand in the position shown in Figure 6-1.
2. Using a non-toxic red or pink magic marker, draw on lips and color them well into the inside of the thumb and first finger. (See Figure 6-2.) You may want to draw the lips on very young children's hands.
3. Make the eyes from scrap paper. Fold a small piece of white paper in half and cut two "footballs" at one time. Add two smaller eye-colored circles with a marker, and black spots in the centers to represent pupils.
4. Attach the eyes to the hand above the mouth with bits of rolled-up masking tape. (See Figure 6-3.)

Try unusual materials 181

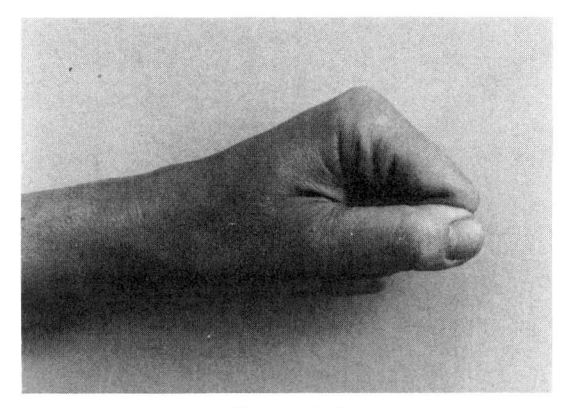

Figure 6-1

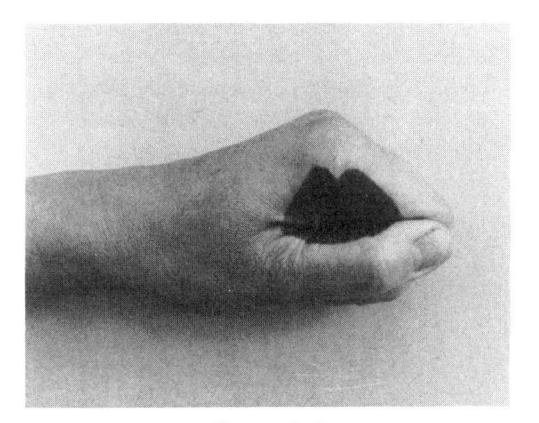

Figure 6-2

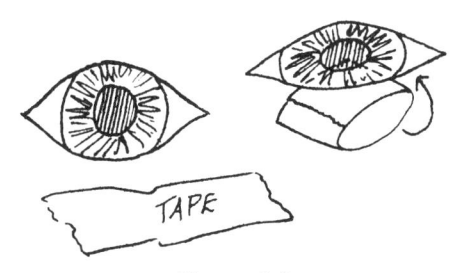

Figure 6-3

5. Add such details as eyelashes, eyebrows, and freckles with thin markers. Make a wig by wrapping yarn around a four- to six-inch piece of lightweight cardboard. Wrap until there is enough yarn for hair. Cut through the middle of the yarn on one side of the cardboard, lay it flat, and tie it tightly with one of the pieces of yarn. (See Figure 6-4.) Roll up a piece of masking tape on the top of the hand above the eyes and attach the wig.

182 *Try unusual materials*

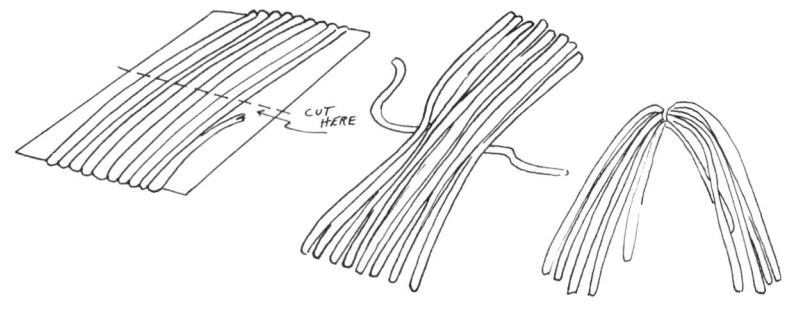

Figure 6-4

6. Complete the puppet with a scrap of cloth as a dress, coat, or cape held in the same hand between other fingers. (See Figure 6-5.)

Figure 6-5

7. Move the mouth of the puppet by keeping the pad of the thumb tight against the second joint of the index finger and moving it up and down, back and forth. The puppet can talk, sing, yawn, eat from a spoon and drink from a straw. Students can use props from around the classroom or make them from scraps of paper.

Uses:

Puppets can be made to go along with stories, plays, or students' creative writing.

You might want shy or troubled students to make two puppets, one on each hand, to encourage interaction and expression with and from themselves.

cute cutoffs
(shirt sleeves as puppet clothes)

Grade Levels: K-3 **Time Needed: 80 minutes**

Before You Begin:

Have each of your students bring in an old shirt to be used as a smock. If the shirt is of "parental vintage," it will have sleeves that are too long for all practical purposes. Instead of throwing those shirt sleeves away after cutting them shorter, show the students how they can be turned into little shirts for small stuffed animals or hand puppets. Depending on the type of shirt, you can make miniature placket-front shirts with collars, turtlenecks, or crew-necked shirts. Show the students a few puppets and animals dressed in shirts so that prior to the lesson they can think of the animals or dolls they will dress.

Objectives:

- To create something from a discard and show its worth.
- To provide a simple hand puppet costume.
- To think creatively.

Materials:

- long-sleeved shirts
- dressmaker's scissors
- stapler
- tape
- small stuffed animals, dolls, or hand puppets
- needles and thread

Procedure:

1. Cut off the sleeves at a length that will provide a shirt body for a puppet, but also leave enough of the sleeve on the shirt as a protection for the upper arms.
2. Cut out two holes from the sides of the shirt body just below the

184 *Try unusual materials*

"collar" for fingers of a hand puppet or the arms of a stuffed animal or doll. Leave the bottom of the shirt straight or cut up on the sides to make "shirttails" for a nightshirt or dress shirt. Make a turtleneck or crew-neck shirt by cutting one sleeve into halves. Make each half into a tube by folding and stapling or stitching it together along the edge. Turn the sleeves inside-out and attach them to the armholes of the shirt by stapling, taping, or sewing. (See Figure 6-6.)

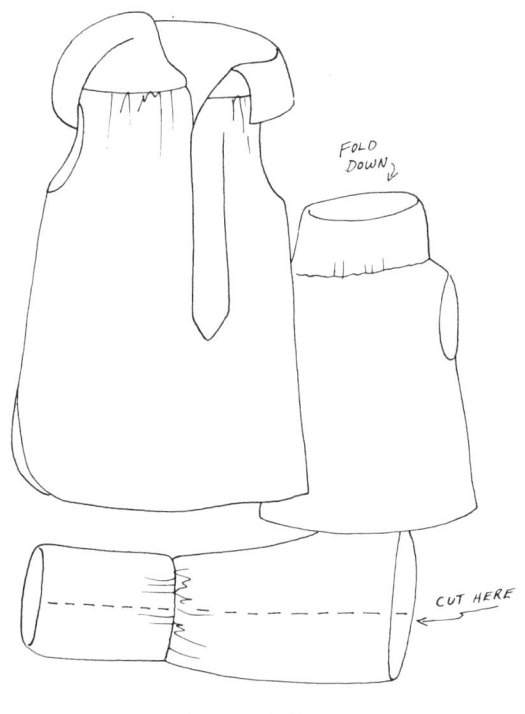

Figure 6-6

3. Clip on a small bow tie or tie, or tie ribbons around the collar. Add jewelry and other decorations, too. Use marking pens on plain colored shirts to design Hawaiian motifs and other patterns.

4. Fit the shirt onto the stuffed animal or doll and see the perfect fit! (See Figure 6-7.)

Variations:

Instead of dressing toys, use a styrofoam ball or cardboard tube to make a head. Make a yarn or paper wig and add a face with buttons,

Try unusual materials 185

Figure 6-7

beads, or markers. Fingers can be used as arms in a sleeveless shirt, and hands can be made of felt or paper scraps and tucked into the sleeves. (See Figure 6-8.)

The shirts can be stuffed, and a sock head and legs added to make a toy; or children might do self-portraits by attaching their shirt to a background and finishing the face and body.

Figure 6-8

Uses:

Puppets can be used to depict characters of a story or nursery rhyme, and might well be used in developing puppet plays for various holidays or events.

Try unusual materials

let your fingers do the talking
(cloth and magazine finger puppet)

Grade Levels: K-6   **Time Needed: 40 minutes**

Before You Begin:

These puppets are an unusual twist on the typical finger puppet because the eyes, mouths, and other details are cut from magazines. These will give the puppets a bizarre character that your students of all ages will find appealing. The most effective motivation is to have a few of these made to show the diverse possibilities available to the students. The puppets are so simple to make that several could be made in a brief amount of time.

Objectives:

- To present a simple means of expression.
- To demonstrate manipulative skills.
- To produce a unique product by combining two-dimensional and three-dimensional elements.

Materials:

- 3" x 6" strips of oaktag
- magazines (fashion and news)
- 12" x 12" cloth scraps
- rubber bands
- glue
- scissors
- dressmaker's scissors
- tape
- ribbon and trim, etc.

Procedure:

1. Cut the 12" x 12" cloth scrap into a 12-inch circle. This need not be accurate.

2. Roll the oaktag strip into a tube three inches high. Be sure the tube fits comfortably over the finger. A thicker tube leaves more room for features.

3. Secure the tube with tape. Then center the cloth over the tube and slip the rubber band over the tube to make it fit tightly at the bottom of the tube. (See Figure 6-9.)

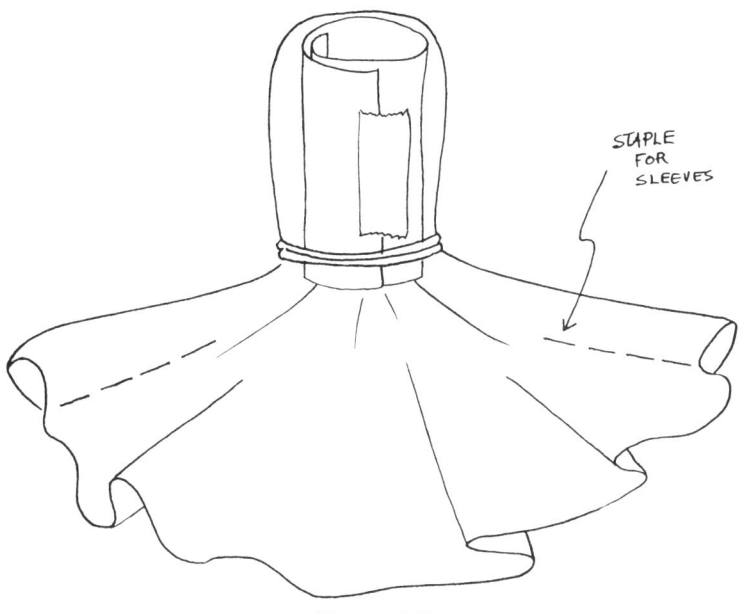

Figure 6-9

4. Search through magazines for the details needed to complete the face. Look for a set of eyes first. These can be cut out to include eyelashes and eyebrows. Attach them with a dab of glue in the middle of each cutout. Keep the three-dimensional effect of the face by allowing the pieces to stick out at the edges.

5. Look for the mouth. Cut smirks or thin-lipped smiles around the outside in a clown-mouth fashion; mouths from fashion magazines are easier to cut out because they are usually well defined with lipstick. Glue the mouth in place, possibly covering the rubber band.

6. Eliminate the nose on this puppet. It is not necessary—and there will probably be no room for one anyway!

7. Finish the puppet with a hat or a ponytail or even something out of place glued to the top of the head. Just remember to cut everything from a magazine, because the realism of the photographs is what gives the puppet character. (See Figure 6-10.)

188 *Try unusual materials*

Figure 6-10

Uses:

These puppets are strictly for fun, so encourage your students to make them anytime! You might have the students vote on the zaniest or the most colorful puppet.

Try unusual materials 189

hooray! I've lost a mitten
(mitten and glove characters)*

Grade Levels: 2-6   **Time Needed: 40 minutes**

Before You Begin:

As winter draws to a close and mittens and gloves are no longer necessary, check your "Lost and Found" box to see what treasures it may offer! You might also ask students if they have any mittens or gloves without mates that they would like to turn into little friends to decorate their desks or sit on a shelf in their rooms. In a few days, you should have enough strays to start this lesson.

Make two or three of the little characters and show your students the possibilities in using either a glove or a mitten to develop a personality. (See Figure 6-11.) Have plenty of scrap trims and materials available so the students can get some ideas by looking through the supplies.

Figure 6-11

---

*First appeared in the November/December 1980 issue of *TEACHER* Magazine. © 1980 *TEACHER* Magazine.

Objectives:

- To use throw-away items to create something worthwhile.
- To increase awareness in the value of common objects as art.

Materials:

- orphaned mittens and gloves
- plastic moving eyes (available from craft supply houses)
- scissors
- glue
- pipe cleaners
- junk jewelry
- scraps of felt and material
- yarn
- ribbon and trim
- pompons
- 6-ounce cans from fruit juice concentrate

Procedure:

1. Stuff the thumb and tip of the mitten with scrap material. If using a glove, stuff the thumb and the hand for fullness. Use the thumb as the nose, and either flop down the rest of the fingers on the glove or stuff them to stick straight out as horns or antennae.
2. Pull the glove or mitten down over the juice can.
3. Glue on the eyes and go absolutely wild from there! Glue pompons on the end of the nose or antennae, or use as earmuffs. Make eyeglasses from pipe cleaners, and add a moustache and beard to make the character exciting. Glue mops of yarn on the mitten top for hair.
4. Cut up extra mittens to form winter hats for the heads. Cut off the tip and roll up the cut edge to form one hat. Then cut off the thumb section so that the wrist can be turned inside out and secured with a rubber band at the cut edge to make a second hat. (See Figure 6-12.)

Figure 6-12

5. Every one will be different... even orphaned mittens can find a home!

Uses:

The finished characters make wonderful models for illustrating. They can be drawn facing each other and speaking in cartoon fashion, using "balloons." (See Chapter 4's "If You Laugh, I'll Cry" for ideas on cartoon illustration.)

Creative writing can also be stimulated by the use of these characters. Unstuffed, they can be used as hand puppets, and characters can be developed to act out a particular story.

it's raining cats and dogs
(clay bead jewelry)

Grade Levels: 4-6 **Time Needed: 80 minutes**

Before You Begin:

Tell the students that they will make clay "beads" to be strung on ribbon or yarn. The faces can even have moving eyes. Show them the patterns for a dog, a cat, and a moon face. Make several faces before the lesson and, of course, demonstrate these for your students, showing them how to use the various tools. They will get the idea very quickly, and be off and running!

Objectives:

- To develop small manipulative skills.
- To develop a knowledge of clay and its use as a decorative finished product.
- To decorate clay, using common items as tools.
- To develop individual expression.

Materials:

- firing clay
- a kiln
- newspaper to cover work area
- small sponge pieces and water
- plastic bags and twisters
- tools (used toothbrushes, butter knives, spoons, popsicle sticks, wooden cotton swabs stripped of cotton, nails, paper clips)
- plastic wiggly eyes (optional)
- watercolors of various colors
- small brushes
- plastic spray finish
- liquid shoe polish in various colors
- soft cloths
- ribbon, yarn, shoelaces, key chains

Procedure:

1. Prepare the clay as described in Chapter 3's "Stamp, Stamp, Stamp." Remember to wedge the clay sufficiently as these clay beads will be thick and the possibility of air pockets will be increased. Prepare a lump of clay that will accommodate several beads 1½ inches in diameter. Divide the clay into a few balls and place them in a plastic bag until needed.

2. Gently hammer each ball into a thick "cookie," using the side of a clenched fist and making sure that the thickness is even and thick enough to be drilled through from side to side to accommodate a chain or ribbon.

3. Once the cookie is prepared, use a butter knife to cut off parts of the clay to form a cat or dog. (See Figure 6-13.) To have a moon face, do not cut anything.

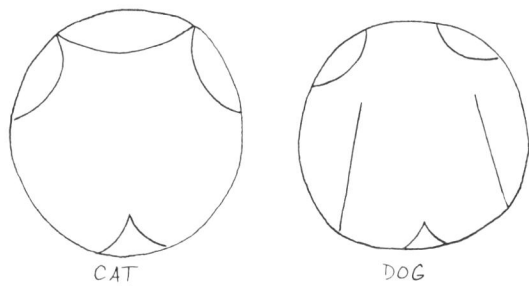

Figure 6-13

4. After cutting the clay away, use a moist sponge to wipe the total edge of the face, rounding off the front and back edges all around the bead. Keep in mind that any burrs of clay left on the bead will become permanent in the firing process, so clean the bead thoroughly with the sponge.

5. Now, start the face. Have some scrap clay handy to use in experimenting with the tools. Try different expressions, using the tools to make eyes, mouths, noses, whiskers, etc. The eyes are most important, so look for items that will yield eye-type impressions. You can produce great eyes on all three faces by using the whole end of the toothbrush handle. Use it slanted for the cat, straight up for the dog, and any which way for the moon face. (See Figure 6-14.) The clay that is forced through the hole can be impressed again with a closed ballpoint pen tip or the cotton swab stick. Wiggly eyes can be glued into the hole after firing.

6. Make the noses the same way or add them on. If additions are used, scratch the area to receive the additional clay with a paper clip or knife tip. (This is called "dagging.") Scratch the ball of clay to be added and then make it slippery with water. (This is called "slipping.") After dagging and slipping, weld the clay pieces together with a spoon tip or popsicle

194   *Try unusual materials*

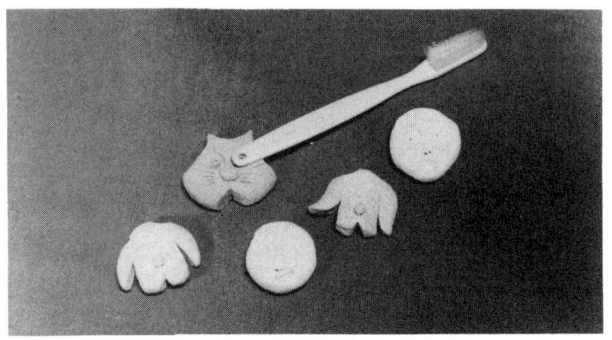

Figure 6-14

stick. (See Figure 6-15.) Another way to make a nose is to pull it up gently from the middle of the cookie before the eyes are impressed. If this is going to be done, leave a high spot in the cookie when hammering it into shape.

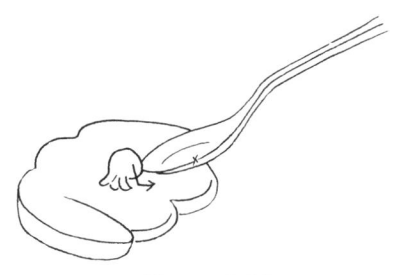

Figure 6-15

7. Use a paper clip to make final details on the faces. Just make sure that the tool is always used to impress—not draw—the details.

8. Drill the hole for the ribbon or chain. If the eyes are to be "moving eyes" for a key chain, make sure the hole is drilled directly behind the eyes. Otherwise, drill through the top section of the dog's head, or through the head below the ears for the cat. Use the wooden cotton swab to make the hole. Holding the bead in the palm of the hand, gently force the stick through the clay from one side to the other. Once it is through, move the stick in a circular fashion until the hole is large enough to receive yarn, ribbon, chain, or whatever will be used as the necklace. Go through the hole from both sides to make sure it is clear and remove any excess clay at the hole sites with a butter knife. If the eyes will be open into this channel, drill them slowly and carefully, constantly removing the bits of clay by going through the side hole and then the eyes. Remember that the clay shrinks in drying, and shrinks more in the firing process, so make sure that the hole for the necklace is sufficient to allow for this shrinkage.

9. Remove any burrs with a sponge and let the pieces air dry thoroughly before firing.

10. Stain the finished beads by polishing them completely front and back with liquid shoe polish. Individual details can be painted with watercolors and tiny brushes. (See Figure 6-16.) Keep in mind that the clay is highly absorbent, so use very little water. Once the paint is applied, it cannot be removed. Use a plastic spray finish to get a glossy patina over the watercolored beads and to protect the clay pieces from fingerprints and smudges. Get a glossy finish on the liquid shoe polish by polishing the beads with a soft cloth.

Figure 6-16

Variation:

Small, round, or oval beads can be added to the main bead by rolling pea-sized balls of clay and forcing the wooden stick through the center to make a hole for the stringing. Roll the ball back and forth on the stick until the hole is large enough. These smaller beads can also be decorated by impressing with the tools—but be sure to keep the ball of clay on the stick until the decorating is complete. String these small beads with the "face" beads on yarn, leather, and ribbon.

Uses:

The beads lend themselves to particular areas of studies, especially ancient history and American history. Have your students design Egyptian or Indian beads and display them in the classroom.

The finished necklaces also make ideal gifts for family members and friends.

196   *Try unusual materials*

hello! we're weaving
(telephone wire mobile)

Grade Levels: 5-6   **Time Needed: 120 minutes**

Before You Begin:

Explain to the students that weaving is a process of going over-under-over in the first row, and then under-over-under in the second. This lesson uses "spider-web" weaving—going around and around from a center. Make an example of the weaving before starting this lesson and show the students the examples in Figures 6-17 and 6-22.

Figure 6-17

Objectives:

- To learn basic vocabulary connected with weaving: warp, weft.
- To practice the basics of weaving.
- To strengthen manipulative skills through construction procedures.

Materials:

- colored telephone wire (available from the local telephone company)
- scrap yarn
- tape
- scissors
- pliers
- costume jewelry, beads, bells
- wire coat hangers. (NOTE: Use the type from a dry cleaning establishment as these are more pliable.)

Procedure:

1. Cut away the casing that covers the multi-colored telephone wire, and separate by removing any winding threads.

2. With pliers, reshape the hook of the hanger to form a small closed loop as a hanging device. Do this first, as a safety procedure.

3. Shape the hanger into a regular (rather than irregular) shape, such as a circle, oval, square, or rectangle. Use pliers to help get rid of kinks or to help form corners, but keep in mind that the hook of the hanger is the hanging device so it should be located at the top of the shape.

4. Stretch two pieces of wire, cut a bit longer than the width of the wire frame, across the frame to divide it into four sections. Wrap the wire around the frame, then twist it down on itself. (See Figure 6-18.) Cut the wire with ordinary school scissors. Gently apply a piece of tape to the connections if they slide on the frame, but the tape will not become a part of the finished product, so it should be put on loosely and taken off as soon as weaving establishes the locations of all of the wires.

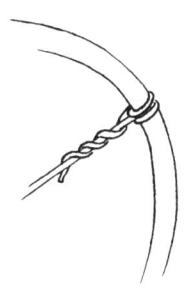

Figure 6-18

5. Continue to divide the frame with wires crossing the center until 16 spaces are made within the frame. (See Figure 6-19.) These 16 wires are called the "warp."

Try unusual materials

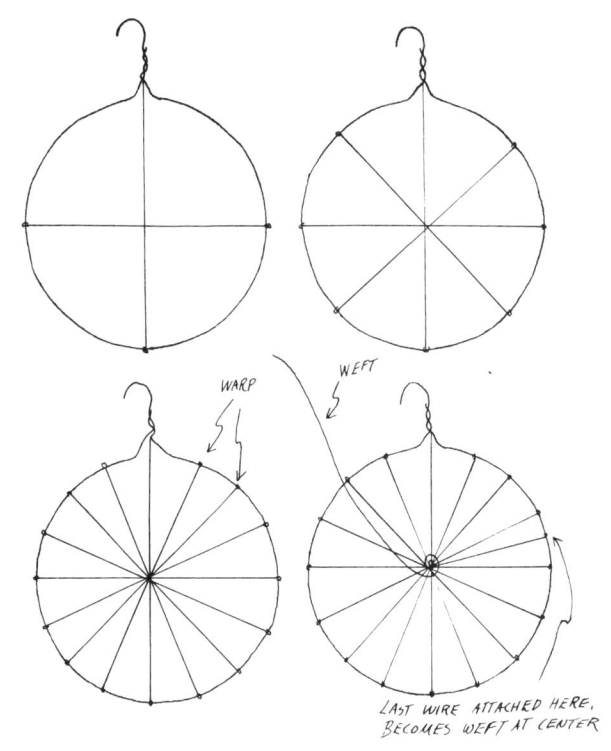

Figure 6-19

6. Make a 17th section by adding one last wire, a long one, to the frame. Attach it to the center by bringing all the wires together and wrapping it through until the center is secured. This is the beginning weaving wire or "weft."

7. Start weaving from the center in a circular fashion, going over one wire and under the next. Keep the weaving wire tight as it goes around, so use a popsicle stick, pencil, or the tips of closed scissors to force the wire toward the center.

8. As the weaving progresses away from the center, slip beads on the wire and arrange them in between the warp wires in a random or organized pattern. As the wire gets shorter, add on another or tie on a piece of yarn. (See Figure 6-20.)

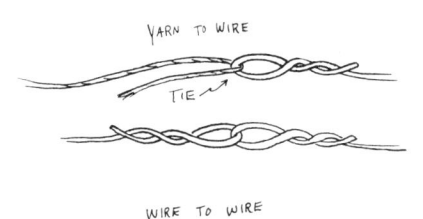

Figure 6-20

9. Elaborate upon the mobile by adding extra loops of wire filled with beads to the entire outside of the frame with connections occurring at each warp attachment or across several sections for larger scallops. The petal-like effect enhances the weaving, even if the whole center has not been filled with weaving. Hang several lengths of wire filled with beads from the bottom sections of the frame, adding items that jingle, clink, rattle, or ring to achieve a wind-chime effect. (See Figure 6-21.)

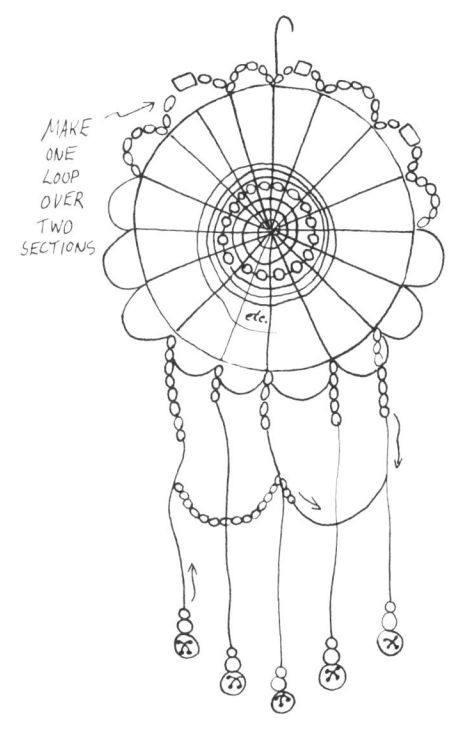

Figure 6-21

Variation:

The activity can be done with scrap yarn if telephone wire cannot be obtained. The beading is more difficult, however, and a needle has to be used throughout the weaving project.

The wire frame may be wrapped with a colorful arrangement of wire or with yarn, using a slip stitch. Even if weaving is not completed, the finished product will have appeal.

Uses:

The finished mobiles often look like Indian designs, so correlate them to history studies. (See Figure 6-22.)

200   *Try unusual materials*

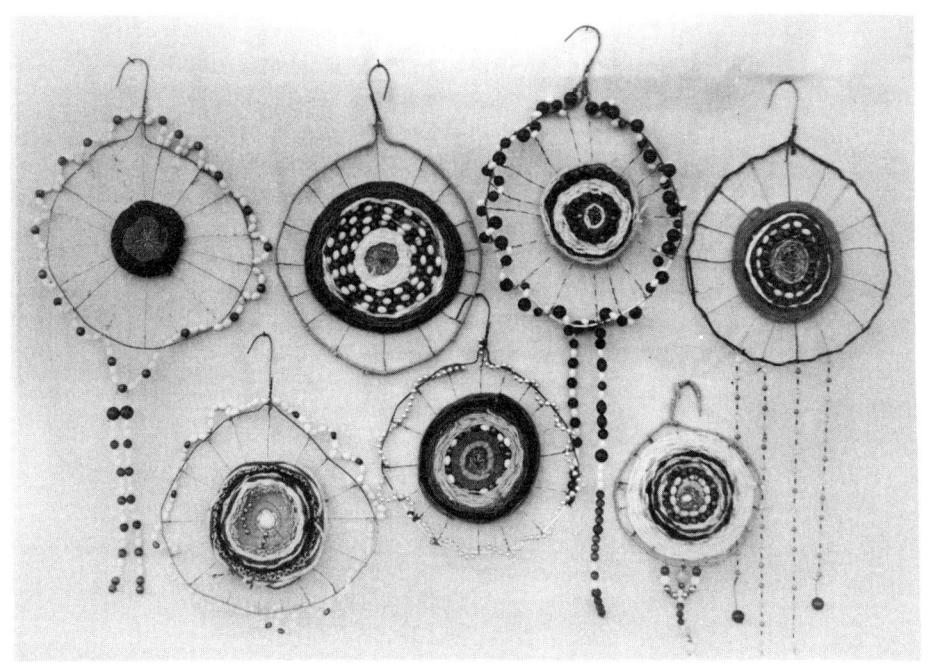

Figure 6-22

The mobiles cast interesting shadows if hung in a sunny window or where they pick up light. The beads, if glass or plastic, will glow, so hang them in windows or close to (but not against) a plain wall.

three-dimensional poetry
(sculptures and creative writing)

Grade Levels: 5-6   **Time Needed: 80-120 minutes**

Before You Begin:

An array of natural materials can motivate your students to create a sculpture, especially if there is plenty to work with. There are no rules since the students will be confined to the base that you provide. They can work flat in a collage-type manner, or they can build upward with the materials. Tell your students to select carefully because they will want to develop a theme or some particular subject to write about. They may want to choose an item or two to build around—a small shell or pod, or perhaps a branch that will be decorated with leaves, shells, or feathers.

It would be effective to show a finished sculpture that is accompanied by two creative writings to demonstrate the directions the students are expected to follow. For instance, if you make a sculpture consisting of rocks and pebbles arranged on a water-colored base with a small frog perched on one of the rocks (see Figure 6-23), you might enhance it with these poems:

(rhyming)	Rocks lie baking in the sun, Water warms in pools; As I dive without a run, Droplets shine like jewels. Won't you join me?
(Haiku)	Should I bathe today? I'd rather sit and watch flies fly close enough.... Gulp!

Objectives:

- To demonstrate the relationship between sculpture and poetry in an art form.
- To encourage simplicity in visual and literary expressions.
- To learn the basics of simple poetry construction.
- To provide an opportunity for creative expression.

Figure 6-23

Materials:

- a base (random wood scraps, cardboard painted or covered with paper, small boxes)
- glue
- natural materials (wood scraps, driftwood, pine cones, twigs, sand, bark, moss, shells, nuts, pods, feathers, beans, seeds, waxed leaves, stones, pebbles, rocks)
- ceramic or plastic figures
- florist's clay
- research books on simple poetry and Haiku
- pencils
- lined paper
- markers
- scrap paper

Procedure:

1. Choose and prepare a base.
2. Gather and arrange, by trial and error, a pleasing sculpture that follows a theme, such as birds and twigs, feathers and shells, twigs and flowers, sand and shells, or choose one item to be the central focus in the arrangement.
3. Glue everything together, using florist's clay in hidden places wherever necessary to hold twigs or other hard-to-hold items in place. Allow plenty of drying time before moving the sculpture.

Try unusual materials 203

4. Write about the sculpture or about the ideas it represents. For instance, rocks may be mountains, a feather may represent a bird, and shells could become the whole ocean! Use either Haiku or a rhyming pattern.

5. Haiku (pronounced *high*-koo) is an ancient form of Japanese poetry that has become a major part of Japanese culture. The poem is set up in three lines consisting of a certain number of syllables in each line. The first line must have five syllables; the second, seven; and the third, five. The requirements hone the writer's thoughts, and results should be simple and crisp. The students may write about the actual sculpture or about the ideas it represents. Here are three examples from *Birds, Frogs and Moonlight,* translated by Sylvia Cassedy and Kunihiro Suetake (Doubleday and Co., Inc., 1967):

> All at once, the storm!
> Overcome, a poor sparrow
> grasps a blade of grass.
>
> Buson

> Old pond, blackly still—
> frog, plunging into water,
> splinters silent air.
>
> Basho

> A discovery!
> On my frog's smooth, green belly
> there sits no button.
>
> Yayu

6. Rhyming poetry is a bit more difficult, but here are a few simple construction forms to follow (the letters in each pattern represent the words that rhyme at the end of the poetry lines):

(1)	(2)	(3)	(4)	(5)
a	a	a	a	a
b	b	a	b	b
a	a	b	——c	c
b	b	b	b	
	z!	c	d	a
c		c	e	b
d		d	——f	c
c		d		z!
d			e	

Put the letters at the end of the lines on scrap writing paper. Fill in the last word in each line according to the theme and rhyme the matching letters. Fill in each line with a sentence or phrase ending in the already established rhyming words. The "z" arrangement represents a "zinger" or something at the end of a line that does not rhyme. It could be a phrase or one word like "Help!" or "Boing!" If this does not work out, change the sentences around to end with different words, or change the rhyming system. Increase the poems in length by repeating the pattern as many times as desired. Each repeat is called a *stanza* and may even be changed in pattern. NOTE: Do not confine students to these patterns. They may invent their own arrangement of rhyming words, too. Next, organize the rhythm. Match—in length, number of syllables, or speaking rhythm—the lines that rhyme with each other. Do this by using the "da-don-dee" method in a sing-song manner. "Da" represents one word and "da-da" can be two syllables from the same or different words.

(example)   Da da da da don,
            Da-da da-da da-dee;
            Da da da da don,
            Da-da da-da da-dee.

(example)   Da-da da-da da-don,
            Da-da da-da da-dee;
            Da-da da-da da-DA da-da
            Da-da da-da da-dee!

7. When the sculpture is finished and the creative writing is ready to be copied, write the poem on heavier unlined paper that can be displayed with the sculpture. Use lined composition paper underneath as a guide to print the poems neatly, and decorate if desired.

Variations:

The sculptures may be as large or as small as base size or space permits. The theme might be centered on a season (spring), an area (the mountains), or to accommodate the materials available. A lot of shells in your supplies may set a "shore" theme. Pine cones by the dozens might establish a woodsy atmosphere. Let the students use their imaginations— and at the same time help clean out the "junk" box!

heigh-ho, the dairy-o, the farmer is a doll
(stuffed doll)

Grade Levels: 5-6   **Time Needed: 160 minutes**

Before You Begin:

Make one of these dolls to show your students. (See Figure 6-24.) NOTE: Before starting the lesson you should review the sewing details for hands, feet, facial features and "jeans" in the marionette lesson at the end of this chapter. Showing the students the finished product should be enough to get them interested in starting to find supplies. A good time to do this lesson is in the spring when family members might be cutting old jeans into shorts for the summer. But any kind of pants will do, and a scarecrow look can be achieved with a combination of patterns for pants and shirts. Makeup, freckles, and a straw hat add to its realism.

Figure 6-24

Objectives:

- To learn basic sewing techniques.
- To create a pleasing product from inexpensive supplies.
- To develop manipulative skills in three dimension.

Materials:

- opaque pantyhose or knee-high stockings
- polyester stuffing
- leg from cutoff jeans. (NOTE: Each student needs only one.)
- needles and thread
- yarn
- dressmaker's scissors
- scrap material
- a sewing machine
- staplers
- felt scraps
- plastic moving eyes (optional)
- makeup and decorative notions (buttons, ribbon, trim, bandana, straw hat)

Procedure:

1. Cut off the feet of two pairs of pantyhose so that there is enough to make the hands and feet, plus a little extra to secure them inside the pants' bottom and shirt sleeves.

2. Stuff the hose and form the hands and feet. Pull the stuffing into round pancake shapes for the hands and longer pads for the feet. Stitch fingers and toes into the hands and feet. (See Figure 6-25.) The number of fingers and toes can be reduced for a cartoon effect and to cut down on the amount of sewing required.

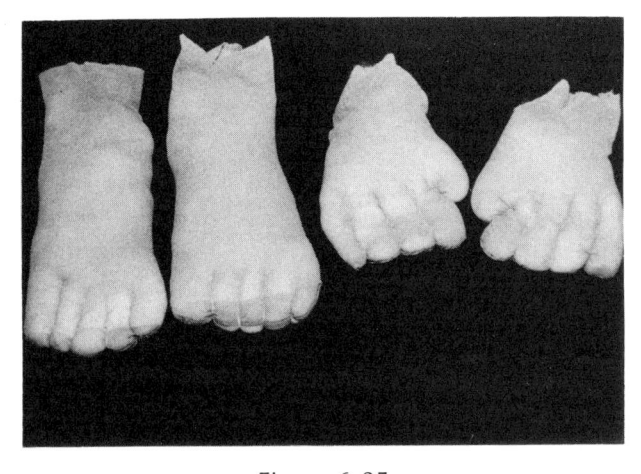

Figure 6-25

3. Make the head from a center section of hose, about eight inches long. This part will more than likely be free of runs, so it would be the best part to use for a face. Tie the end of the tube of hose into a knot, turn it inside out, and stuff it to form a good-sized head.

4. For older students, use the suggested features ideas in the marionette lesson to complete a face. Younger children can use scrap material to cut out a mouth and nose, and glue these to the face. Sew eyebrows in with yarn or draw them on with a marking pen. Glue on felt circles or plastic moving eyes. Buttons can also be sewn in place for noses and eyes. Add some felt freckles and blush on the cheeks and lipstick for a mouth that has been sewn.

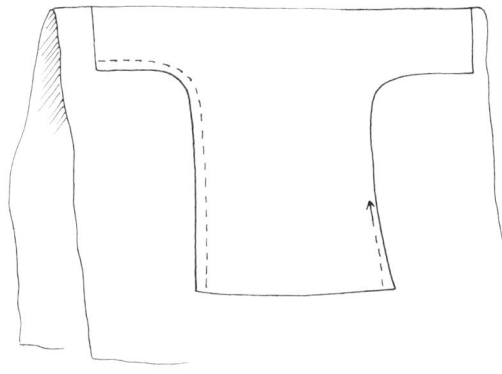

Figure 6-26

5. Make a yarn wig by wrapping yarn around a small book until you have a good amount. Cut the yarn off and tie it in the middle to make a "mop." After it is stitched or glued to the head, the wig can be cut, tapered, cut into bangs, braided, or tied into ponytails. Add ribbons, a bandana, a small hat, or a moustache made from some of the yarn.

6. Turn the jeans' legs inside out and cut up the middle to form a small pair of jeans. Either on a sewing machine or by hand, sew the inside seam of the pants and clip at the top of the in-seam. "Farmer jeans" are described in the marionette lesson and can be used for this project.

7. Make a shirt with very little sewing, but be sure it is sewn together solidly enough to hold the stuffing. Use the finished jeans as a guide to make a shirt pattern. (See Figure 6-26.) Be sure the width of the shirt pattern at the bottom is 1½ inches more than the width of the pants' waist. After sewing, clipping the seam under the arms, and turning, fit the shirt over the pants or into the pants.

8. Insert the hands and feet and sew or staple across the pants and sleeves to secure them in place. Stuff the pants and shirt with scrap material or polyester stuffing. Put the two parts together, and stitch closed. Add a bit of rope or twine as a belt.

9. Snip a small hole at the top of the shirt to insert the neck. Stitch or staple the loose stocking of the head in place, then add a scarf cut from scrap material to cover the connection.

10. Add any other details necessary to help develop the character of the doll. Try putting patches on the pants or adding back pockets.

Uses:

These dolls can be used for creative writing. Give the characters names and then write stories or poems about them. What do they do for a living? Where do they live? What is their life like along the Mississippi?

The dolls can also be used as room decorations, pillows, or gifts for a younger friend or family member.

Try unusual materials 209

more and more books
(marbleized paper notebooks)

Grade Levels: 5-6   **Time Needed: 40 minutes**
(for marbleizing)
80 minutes
(for bookmaking)

Before You Begin:

This lesson only needs the marbleizing demonstration to excite your students into action. As far as the actual bookmaking is concerned, you will demonstrate this at a second session when the marbleized papers have dried. If you want to try the process ahead of time, you can make a few books to give the students an idea of how the finished products will look. (See Figure 6-27.) The "true" marbleizing experience should be described to the students so that they can do this project on their own, if they have an opportunity.

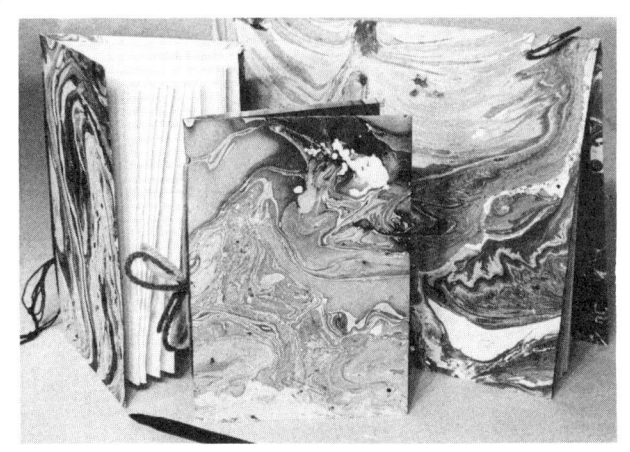

Figure 6-27

Objectives:

- To introduce a new technique of painting and decorating.
- To reinforce manipulative skills with emphasis on precision.
- To present a simple bookbinding technique using mitered corners.
- To provide an opportunity for success with a pleasing finished product as a result.

Try unusual materials

Materials:

(for marbleizing)
- 9" x 12" construction paper in assorted colors. (NOTE: Size depends on the size of the water containers you will use.)
- white vellum drawing paper
- manila paper
- assorted enamel or oil-based paints
- popsicle sticks or tongue depressors
- screwdriver
- turpentine or hand cleaner
- cloths
- old baking pans, cookie sheets, or any shallow containers that will hold water and accommodate 9" x 12" or larger paper
- paint shirts. (NOTE: Students should be encouraged to wear old clothing for this lesson.)
- newspapers to completely cover work area

(for bookmaking)
- 9" x 12" oaktag
- scissors
- 9" x 12" construction paper in assorted colors. (NOTE: Increase paper sizes if marble paper is larger.)
- white glue
- scissors
- brushes
- paper
- hole punch
- yarn
- cloth or electrical tape (optional)

Procedure:

1. Be sure the work area and all clothing are completely covered and protected. This lesson requires less cleanup if it can be done outdoors.

2. Put three or four paint cans by each pan to be used. Place a tongue depressor or popsicle stick by each paint can. Hide the lids somewhere else so they will be clean and available for closing the cans at the end of the session. Spread the wealth of colors by putting "blah" paints at each pan; brown, white, black, beige, and gray can be exciting if used with a bright color, such as yellow, red, purple, blue, or orange.

3. Set out a selection of construction paper along with a few crayons. Initial one side of the paper as soon as the color is chosen. This helps in identifying the marbleized paper later.

4. Add a layer of cold water to each pan so that it is just below the top of the pan.

5. "Float" some paint of each color on the water by applying the paint with the stick in a circular, dripping fashion—*without touching the water with the stick*. Keep the respective sticks with the cans they belong to, either in or next to each one. Use an extra stick as a mixer to "marbleize" the paint on the water by stirring and swirling the paint. When the right composition is made, it is ready to be captured on paper! NOTE: True marbleizing needs more than just a quick swirl to mingle the colors. If time allows, let the paints marbleize by themselves. This will happen if the paint is left alone to intermingle by a chemical process. The different colors and also the variety of brands of paint will cause this process to develop intricate patterns that cannot be done with the mixing stick. Be sure to mention this to students. They may want to set up their own area at home to do marbleizing, but in the classroom, encourage them to keep their eyes on the pans and pick up prints *between* applications of paint. All students will want to put their own paint on the water, but the residual left by a student will provide a beautiful design without adding more paint.

6. Drop the construction paper into the pan with the initial-side up. Make sure all four corners of the paper touch the water and there are no air pockets lumped up in the middle. Touch gently with fingertips but do not submerge the paper.

7. Pick up the paper from one side and quickly flip it over to be carried on flat open-palmed hands to the designated drying area. Only water will drip from the paper if the paint application was not done heavily. Discourage dripping the paper off into the pan because all of the paint will run in one direction and the marbleized effect will be lost.

8. Clean up by pouring the water in the pans into large cans to be discarded, but not before picking up all the marbleizings that will continue to happen. If possible, leave the pans overnight and, the next day, just pick off the skins of paint that will form. This is not so messy a clean-up, as there will only be clear water left at that point.

9. At the next session, start the books. Cut oaktag down to 8" x 11" to accommodate the 9" x 12" marbleized papers. Choose 7¾" x 10¾" liner papers. Use a paper cutter to prepare assorted colors for students to coordinate with marbleized papers.

10. Fold the marbleized paper, the oaktag, and a liner paper exactly in half to form the "spine" of the notebook. Apply glue with a brush to the marbleized paper along the spine and insert the oaktag, pressing it flat and matching the spines. Give it a chance to dry before trimming at the spine and four corners. (See A in Figure 6-28.) Be sure that the oaktag is not cut, but only the marbleized paper a tiny bit beyond the oaktag corners. The V's near the spine are cut out for ease in folding the book.

212 *Try unusual materials*

11. Slowly fold the marbleized paper margins over the oaktag all the way around. After folding each section up and over, apply a thin layer of glue with a brush to the back of the marbleized paper, where it will fold over onto the oaktag. (See B of Figure 6-28.) Do one section at a time, holding it in place with spread fingertips until dried. Ease the corners together so that no cardboard shows between the meetings of the marbleized paper. Gently fold the book closed while the glue is still damp so the book goes into a closed position easily.

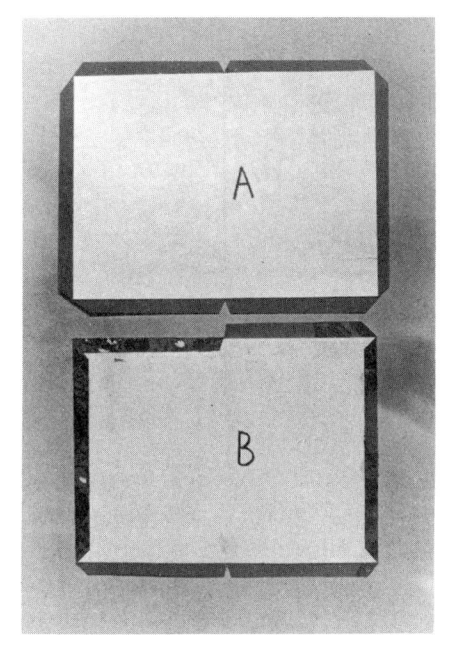

Figure 6-28

12. Insert the liner at the spine first. Then, with the book partially closed, slip in a piece of newspaper and apply glue to the rest of each side of the liner just around the edges, using the newspaper as protection. (See Figure 6-29.) Smooth each side of the liner into place from the spine center, outward, with the book semi-closed. This avoids wrinkles that might occur if the liner were applied to a flat, opened book.

13. Cut several sheets of insert paper to a size slightly smaller than the liner paper, and fold in half to make two pages from each sheet.

14. Punch two holes on the spine so that yarn can be inserted through the middle of a folded packet of paper. (See Figure 6-30.) Put in one piece of paper and mark for the holes. Then punch the rest.

15. Use yarn to tie the pages. Braid the yarn in colors to complement the marbleized cover, use several strands of the same or different colored

Try unusual materials 213

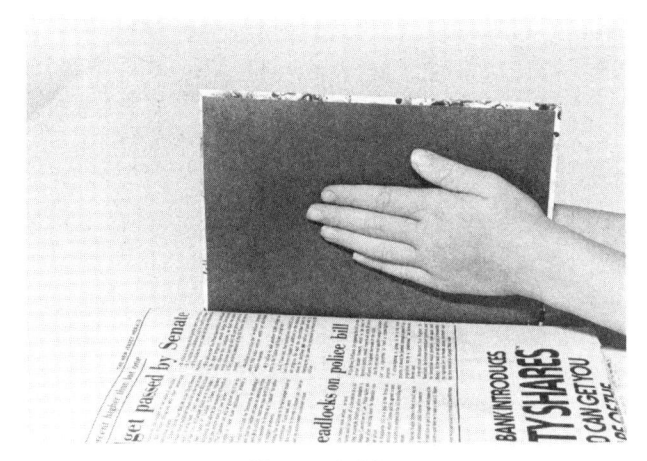

Figure 6-29

Figure 6-30

yarn to get a tassel effect when tied, or add extra loops of yarn so that the book can be hung up near a telephone or desk.

16. Add more paper when needed by untying the yarn.

17. If cracking occurs along the spine on the front of the marbleized paper due to the stiffness of the enamel paints, apply cloth tape or electrical tape before the liner is glued in place. Apply the strip of tape along the spine and fold it over onto the back at the top and bottom. Then glue the liner in place and proceed with inserting pages.

Variations:

Larger books can be made by increasing all paper sizes. For more permanency, although the paint does preserve the paper for future use, the books may be laminated, library book fashion, or possibly the marbleized paper might be laminated *before* the books are made. In this case, make sure there is plenty of margin for gluing the paper to the oaktag—at least one-half inch.

NOTE: The bookmaking process can be followed through with other decorative paper, such as wallpaper and wrapping paper.

Uses:

The marbleized papers can be used as mats to frame sketches, photos, and three-dimensional paper sculptures. Just cut the desired size opening out of the center by using a template or by measuring. Fold on the template line and clip. Then ease in scissors and cut out the center. This perfect smaller piece can then be used to make a smaller book, or it can be cut up and used for collage work. The marbleized paper might also be used to cover cans and boxes, or as wrapping paper.

Finished books make wonderful notebooks for photographs, autographs, sketches, recipes, addresses, telephone numbers, shopping lists, and much more!

who's that?
(foam masks and head gear*)

Grade Level: 6 **Time Needed: 80 minutes**

Before You Begin:

Demonstrate this lesson on a student volunteer by showing a few assembly techniques and discussing the types of details and features that can be made to form the mask. You might have a few different samples made up to show your students the variety of techniques that can be used to put the mask together.

Objectives:

- To provide for interaction with peers in a productive and creative manner.
- To develop skills, such as solving connective problems and devising three-dimensional features, in soft sculpture.

Materials:

- scraps of sheet foam (used for padding under wall-to-wall carpeting)
- scissors
- staplers
- mirror (optional)

Procedure:

1. Students choose partners to help each other measure the proper size rectangle to wrap around the head. If students work alone, a mirror is helpful.

2. Cut a face-mask type of hole in the foam. This hole could have a hinged-door or jail-window effect. The long sides might be cut into fringe, points, or scallops. (See Figure 6-31.)

---

*First appeared in the April 1979 issue of *School Arts*.

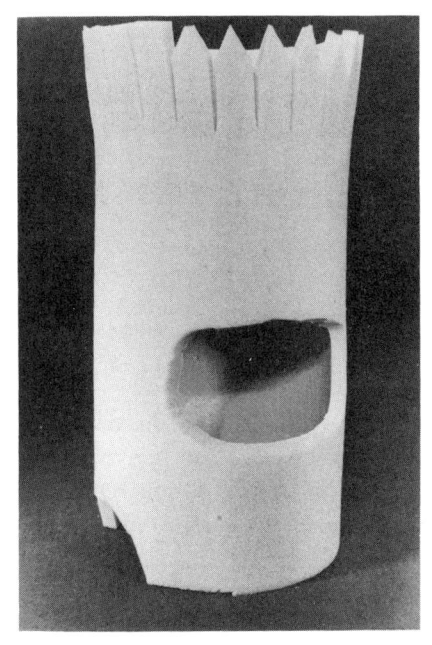

Figure 6-31

3. Staple the sides together and then add details. Cut and tuck ears into tiny slots, or add other decorative details, such as antennae, fangs, tongues, noses, teeth.

4. Experiment with ways to put the foam pieces together by not using any tools other than scissors and stapler. Tie with strips through two slots, weave, braid, notch, and even "sew" with strips of foam through precut holes. (See Figure 6-32.) Some masks can become helmets by the addition of a top piece.

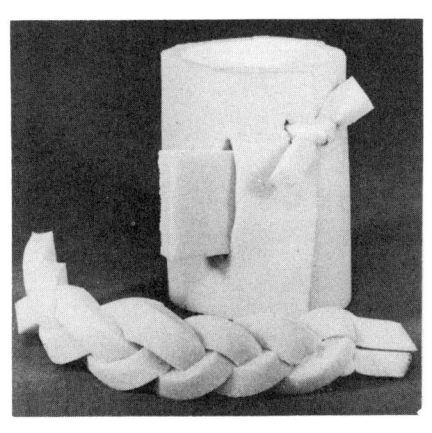

Figure 6-32

Variations:

Your students may want to work in color. Dye the foam by mixing non-toxic liquid tempera with water in a bucket or can, until the desired shade is reached. Dip the foam in the dye, squeeze it out, and let it dry by hanging somewhere where drips won't matter. Then follow the procedure.

Uses:

Use the masks as props for skits with dialogue or movement. The masks might represent a mood.

The masks might also be complete enough to be displayed without the students' heads in them! (See Figure 6-33.)

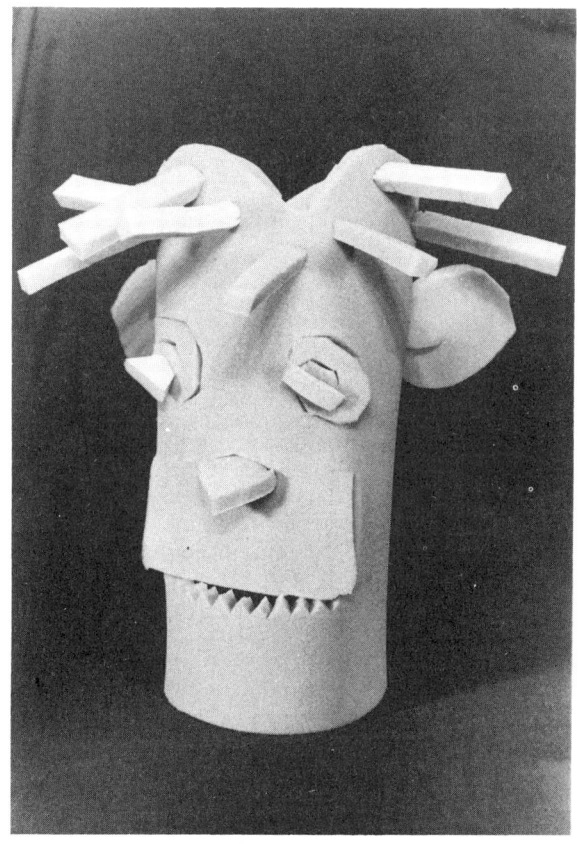

Figure 6-33

218 *Try unusual materials*

I'm almost as big as you are!
(stocking marionettes)

Grade Level: 6   **Time Needed: ten to twelve 40-minute periods**

Before You Begin:

Take the time prior to this lesson to make a marionette. Then walk it around your classroom and let the students examine the details of its realistic appearance. (See Figure 6-34.) This will be enough motivation to interest your students! (The total time for you to construct one, complete with details, may be about three hours.) Give the students a time schedule for gathering supplies, and start the lesson when they have the necessary items.

Figure 6-34

Objectives:

- To develop personal responsibility.
- To increase skills in manipulative areas.

Try unusual materials 219

- To provide an opportunity for physical and oral expressions.
- To learn basic sewing techniques.
- To expand creative thinking and productivity.
- To recognize recycling as an art form.
- To learn to operate and express through a marionette.

Materials:

- two pairs of pantyhose. (NOTE: Hosiery companies may send rejects if requested.)
- an old sock
- a carrier to store supplies (an old purse, duffel bag, laundry bag, beach bag, large shoebox)
- wig or hairpiece (one wig will do for five puppets)
- four paint stirrers or similar sticks, 8" to 10" in length
- worn or outgrown toddler clothing (a dress, overalls, T-shirt, shoes)
- junk jewelry, makeup, items for marionette to hold to develop character (a small piece of sports equipment, musical instrument, bouquet of plastic flowers, small stuffed animal)
- polyester fiber-fill (about three bags will cover 25 to 30 puppets)
- extra hosiery cut into 8" lengths
- rubber bands
- stapler
- tacks
- dressmaker's scissors
- jumbo paper clips
- safety pins
- needles and thread (tan or flesh)
- string or fishing line
- glue
- plastic egg-shaped containers from pantyhose
- ½" moving eyes
- a rope or light chain across classroom
- miniature gum pieces
- sewing machine (if available)

Procedure:

1. Form the torso, arms, and legs, using the two pairs of pantyhose. Stuff all four toes with the fiber-fill, but if shoes will be put on the character, stuff those toes with crumpled newspaper.

2. Put together the two pairs of hose. (See Figure 6-35.) Shove the whole top of one pair into the top of the other pair, leaving only the legs draping out of the top at both sides of the waistband. Make sure the seams are together on the pair of hose that will be the body and legs. Tuck the "arms" in at the "shoulders" or waistband until the hands hang at a proper length, or just above the "knees" of the bottom pair of hose.

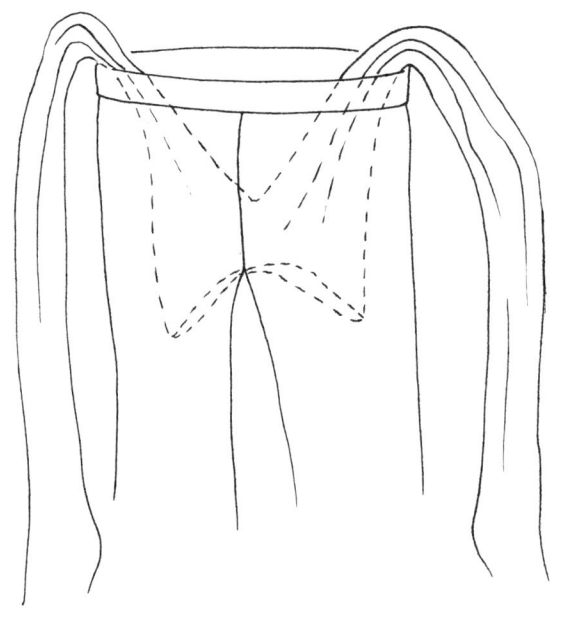

Figure 6-35

3. Lay the torso down flat and insert one shoulder-width stick (about 8 inches long) inside the waistband, with the arms gathered into each end at the proper position. Staple or tack the stick into place at both ends and on both sides of the stick so that nothing slips out of position. (See Figure 6-36.)

4. Use the extra piece of stocking for the head. Gather and secure it in place with a rubber band. Or tie it in a knot at one end, turn inside out, and stuff with a softball-sized wad of fiber-fill. Stretch the bottom of the stocking piece out flat with the stuffing extending down into the "neck" area. Staple it onto the stick by slipping it under the waistband at the center front. (See Figure 6-36 again.)

5. Now cover the neck connection with a sock. Use the top section of the sock, down to the ankle. Cut it straight across and turn it inside out. Cut up from the raw edge on each side about 1½" to 2". (This varies with the size of the sock.) Fold down the top to form a turtleneck and slip the whole piece over the head with the slits drawn over the stick and stretched

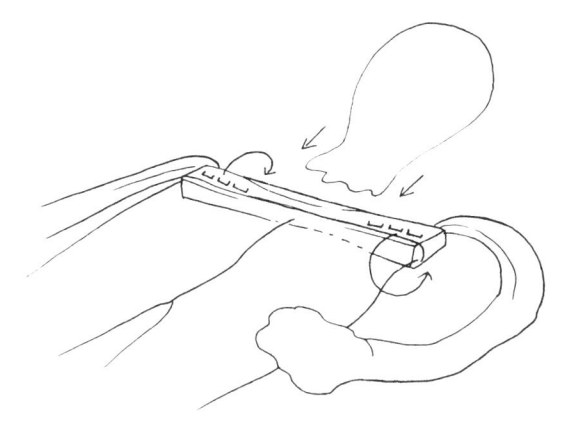

Figure 6-36

out toward the shoulders on both sides of the stick. Staple in place on both sides of the torso. (See Figure 6-37.) NOTE: Now basic clothing, except shoes, can be put on the marionette. Leg and arm lengths can be adjusted to fit the clothing by stapling. Also, without some identification, all of them will look the same. Name tags will also help.

Figure 6-37

6. To make the fingers and toes, gently pull at the stuffing through the stocking and arrange it into a thick pancake shape. Let the pads hang down by holding the marionette up by the shoulders, then pull out a section to form a thumb at the inside front of each "hand." Secure this with a wrap stitch. (See Figure 6-38.)

7. After wrap-stitching the thumb in place, make a knot. Then slip the needle through at the knot site and come up between what will be the first and second fingers. Do a back stitch to form the line between the two fingers. Take care to turn the hand back and forth to make sure all stitches

222   Try unusual materials

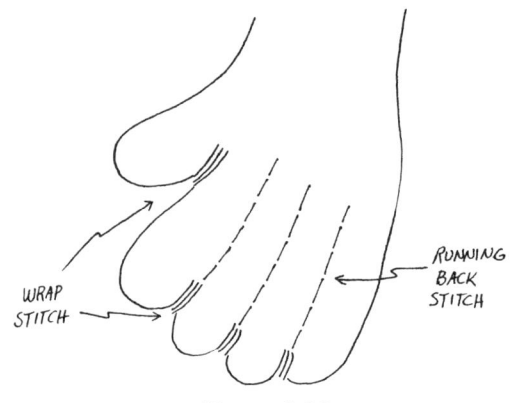

Figure 6-38

line up as closely as possible. (See Figure 6-38 again.) A lot of mistakes can be hidden in the puffiness of the stuffing!

8. At the ends of the fingers, again do a wrap-stitch to form a division between them, slip the needle through at the wrap-stitch site, and come up at the next division between fingers and wrap-stitch. Now, just sew back toward the inside end of the fingers. Continue until all fingers are completed. Toes are sewn in the same manner.

9. Begin the face. Establish the nose first so that the eyes and mouth can be located above and below it. Pull up a bit of stuffing in the center of the ball and, while holding it, stitch the lump into place. Sew back and forth through the base of the nose against the cheeks from top to bottom. Then wrap-stitch around the bottom of the nose and knot. A more realistic nose may be made with diagonal stitching to create nostrils. (See Figure 6-39.)

10. If a clown nose is preferred, cut a double piece of stocking about 2" x 2". Put a bit of stuffing in the center, gather up the corners, and make a sack. Stitch through the gathered neck of the sack, wind the thread around several times, and make a knot. Leave the thread attached while trimming off excess stocking. Turn this part down as the nose is placed on the face and stitch it in place. Use tiny stitches in first the face and then the nose. Secure with a knot when the nose is sewn completely around. (See Figure 6-40.)

11. To make the mouth, gently dig a hole in the stuffing almost to the back of the head. Knot the thread and sew through from back, out of the mouth and back in again. After several stitches, knot the thread on the back of the head. (See Figure 6-39 again.)

12. Elaborate upon the same basic mouth by sewing lips at the top and bottom of the open mouth. Just squeeze some stuffing into lip position

Try unusual materials 223

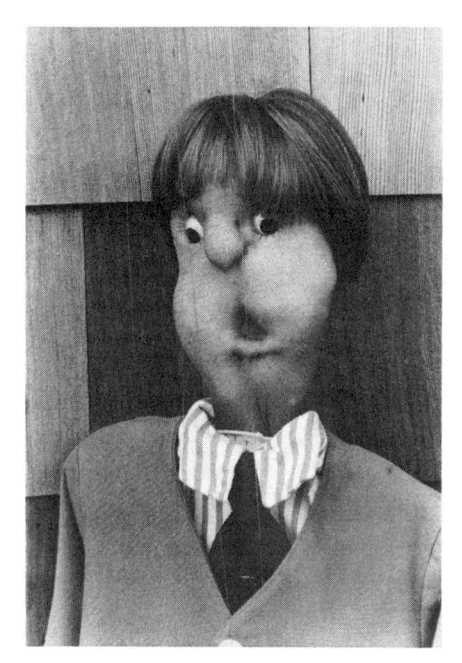

Figure 6-39

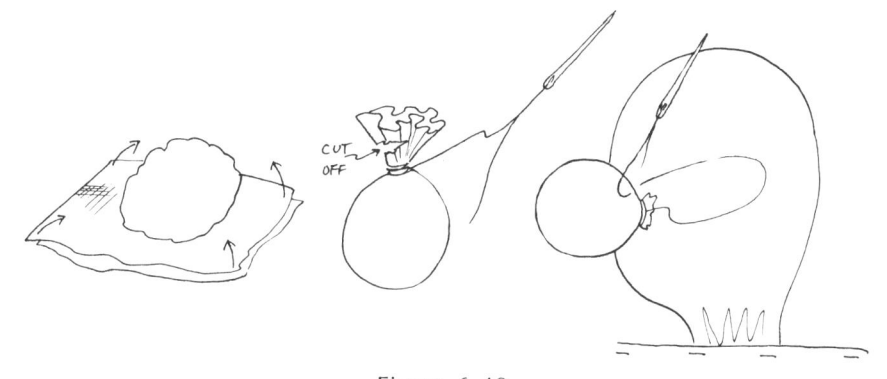

Figure 6-40

and sew it in place with a running stitch. Develop smiles and dimples by molding the stuffing and putting a few stitches here and there. Try different facial expressions, too. (See Figures 6-41 and 6-42.)

    13. Scratch the backs of the plastic eyes with a needle to make them rough. Put a dot of glue on each one and position them on the face. When the glue has dried, stitch them in place. Start with knotted thread and, coming in from the back of the head, bring the needle up at the inside of the eye, near the base of the nose. Sew a running stitch around in a circle, a bit bigger than the size of the eye. Be sure the stitches are small and close

224   *Try unusual materials*

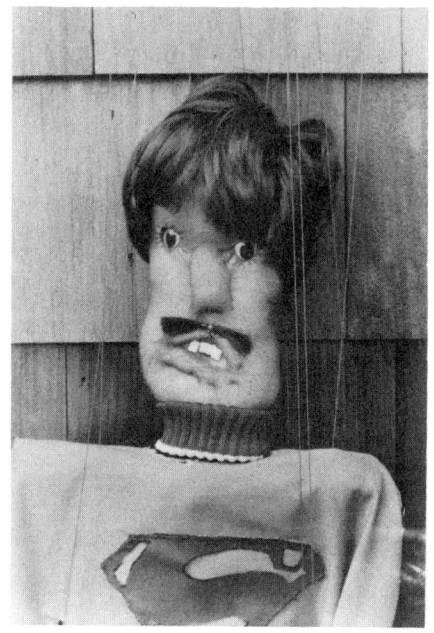

Figure 6-41

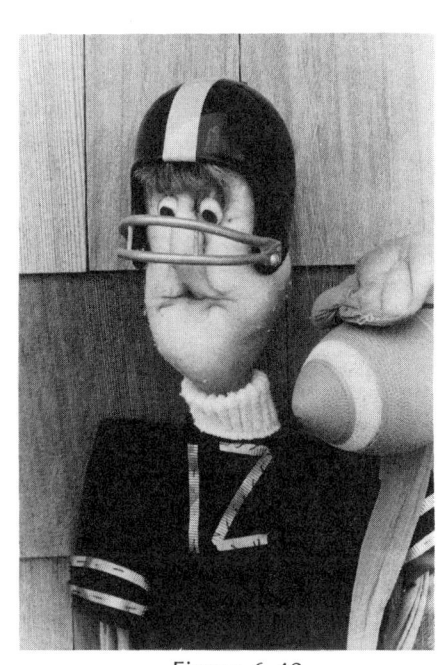

Figure 6-42

together. When you have completely sewn around the eye, pull the thread to gather it. Hold the gathering and eye in place and make a few tiny stitches to secure it from slipping. Then make a knot. (See Figure 6-43.) NOTE: For all sewing, hide the tail of the thread by stitching the needle through to the back of the head after knotting. Then cut the thread.

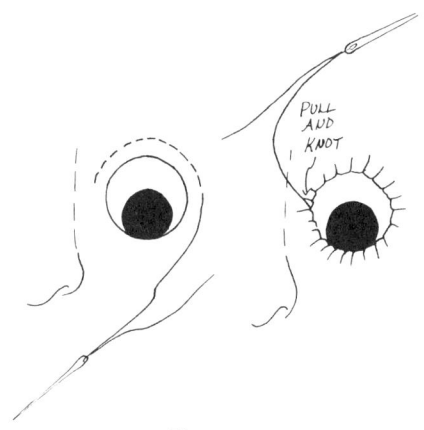

Figure 6-43

14. Stitch small hairpieces onto the head here and there around the edge of the backing. If using a full wig, cut it into smaller ones. Turn a wig inside out and look at the inside. Cut the round section out for one small wig. Cut the rest of the wig into sections across the webs or following the connection lines that go in circles. Cut curved rectangular pieces that will accommodate various sized heads. Fold the piece in half, inside out, and staple or stitch across the top open section. (See Figure 6-44.) Turn it out for a small wig with a part. Stitch the wig in a few places on the head with a wrap-stitch so it will not slip.

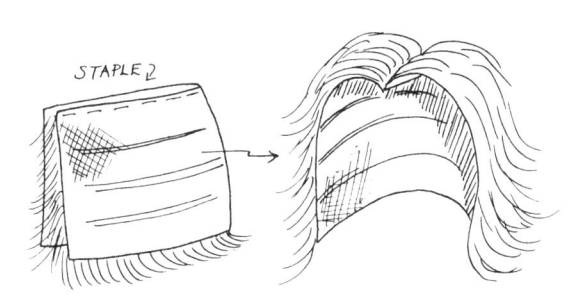

Figure 6-44

226   *Try unusual materials*

15. To use a plastic egg-shaped container on a female puppet, slip two halves that match in size into an extra length of stocking or an old sock. Twist the sock in the middle, and then staple both ends of the stocking onto the torso. (See Figure 6-45.) Use a safety pin to hold the middle twist in place.

Figure 6-45

16. Now, put on the clothes. If they are a bit large, turn them inside out and stitch or staple to make them smaller. Stitch, pin, or staple the clothes to the torso and to each other in obscure places to keep everything together. Dresses or shirts that hang over pants do not need to be secured.

17. To make a pair of jeans that can be used with a small T-shirt, blouse, or baby shirt, use pants legs. Farmer jeans with a bib front are also easy to make, but be sure the leg is long enough to accommodate the puppet's height from the neck down. (See Figure 6-46.) If a shirt is needed, see the suggestion in the "Farmer Doll" lesson, for a simple pattern.

18. Be sure the sticks have the holes in the proper places. (See Figure 6-47.) Sticks 1 and 2 are permanently crossed, so put a bit of glue beween them and lash them together with yarn or string. Open up a jumbo paper clip to form a hook and slip one end under the strings. (See Figure 6-48.)

19. Make sure the sticks are arranged in the manner shown, with the two holes of stick 2 pointing in the same direction as the puppet's nose and the one hole at the back. The three holes in stick 2 are used for the hands, knees, and posterior. The four holes in stick 1 are for the head (inside) and shoulders (outside). (See Figure 6-48 again.)

20. To begin stringing the marionette, hang the puppet (by the paper clip) from a hook, the back of a chair, or a window ledge.

21. String the shoulders first. The weight of the clothes should be

Try unusual materials 227

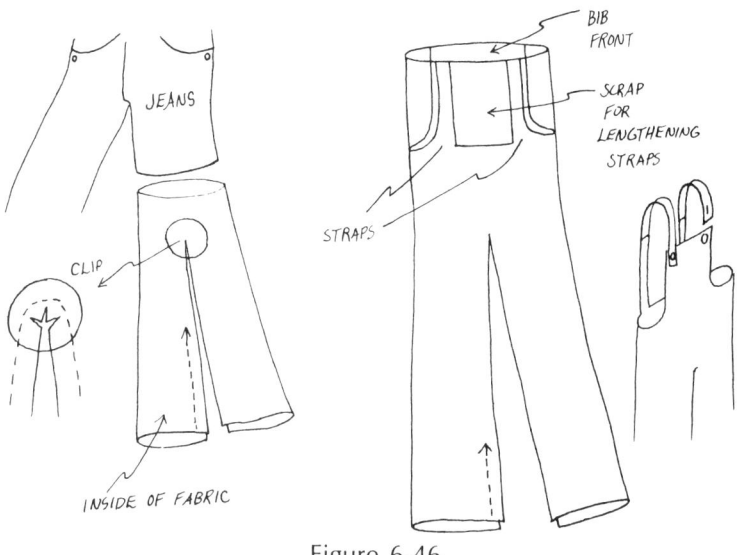

Figure 6-46

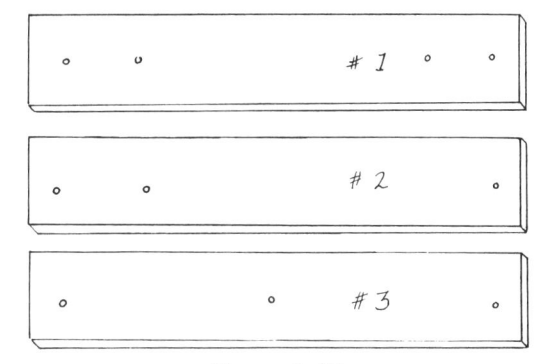

Figure 6-47

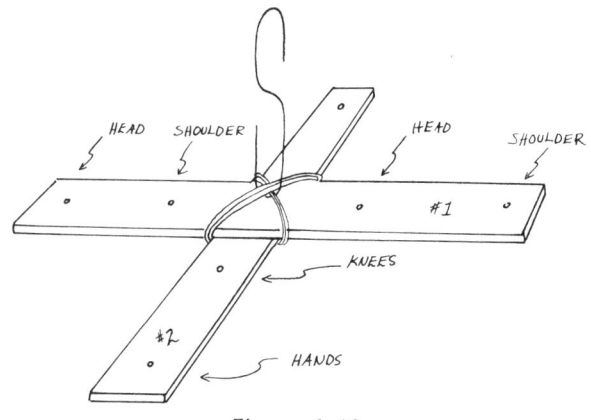

Figure 6-48

taken up by the shoulder stick, so thread a large-eyed needle with about a yard and a half of fishing line or string. Place the needle inside the clothes and insert it under the shoulder stick below one shoulder. Then bring the needle up through all of the clothes and out of the top of the shoulder. The knot will assume the weight of the marionette, but only a string coming out of the shoulder will be seen. Now, go up through the outside hole of stick 1 and down through the opposite hole. Reverse the process and end by making a knot that will catch around and under the shoulder stick. If working wih fishing line, knots will have to be made by tying. String can be knotted at the ends in big knots to support weight.

22. Knot the head string, and then insert it wih a needle through the back of the head. Push it up through the wig on one side of the top of the head. Go through the two remaining holes in stick 1, then back down through the wig and out the back of the head. Mark with the thumb where a knot should be made, then cut off excess string a little below that point. The head should hang straight between the shoulder strings. Release the weight on the string and make a big knot. When it is let go, the head should be in the proper position. (See Figure 6-41 again.)

23. String the knees through the inside hole of the forward-pointing stick (2). This will enable the marionette to sit down or go up steps. Run one string through the knee from the back, up through the hole, down to the front of the other knee, and out the back. Knot the string so that the knees are not pulled up when the marionette is in a hanging position. (See Figure 6-49.) If the marionette is wearing a short dress or has exposed legs, just go through the pantyhose. If the legs are too long, either knot the hose up or staple it well up under the clothes to shorten. Sometimes the shoes will pull the stockings down after hanging for a while, so this may be necessary before the feet are strung. NOTE: At any point after the shoulders are strung, the marionette may be hung for storing. A rope, knotted at intervals to prevent hooks from sliding together, can be strung across the classroom. This will also display marionettes individually.

24. Next, string the hands through the foremost hole in stick 2. Just as for the knees, use one string continuously through both hands. The arms should hang down at the marionette's sides when not in use. Insert the needle near the thumb area on the palm. In this way, the hands will raise in a normal manner with thumbs up. Finish by coming through the back of the other hand and knot off on the palm. (See Figure 6-49 again.)

25. String the seat of the puppet so that it can bend over. Do this by making a knot on a short length of string and inserting the needle only through the pantyhose body. From the front, go inside the shirt or under the dress to set the knot, then through the clothes and out through the seat of the marionette. Tie this string to the last hole left on stick 2.

Try unusual materials

Figure 6-49

26. String the feet on the third stick. Operate this stick a few inches above the crossed sticks, so the line should be measured from the feet up to the stick being held in position. Tie the string to shoelaces or stitch through the stocking or shoe material. Cut the two strings at once so that both feet will be at the same height. (See Figure 6-50.) Just tie the strings to the foot stick, then roll up the slack and attach the center hole over the bottom hook of the paper clip hanger. (Hang the marionette in this way when not in use.)

27. Now that the stringing is complete, put the final details on the face. Regardless of the sex of the marionette, use makeup on the face. A bit of blusher on the cheeks is essential and the mouth needs some color. Use miniature gum pieces that have been spray painted white for teeth. Glue them in place with a bit of glue that has been exposed to the air for a while. The gum pieces are easier to hold in place if the glue is somewhat tacky. Stitch in eyebrows with yarn or thread, or draw on with a marker or an eyebrow pencil. False eyelashes might also be glued on.

28. Allow your students to create their own puppets, letting the character of each puppet emerge as a result of available supplies or ingenuity on the part of the more involved students. The finished puppets will be varied and very exciting! (See Figures 6-51 through 6-55.)

Operation of the marionette requires a little practice, and if two or three students work together, they can help each other with the action.

230 *Try unusual materials*

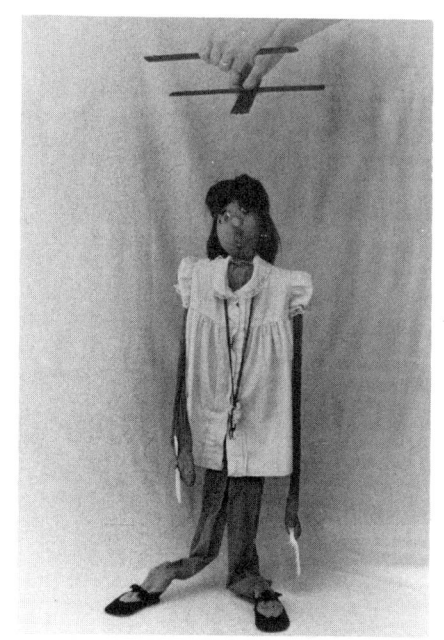

Figure 6-50

Figure 6-51

Try unusual materials 231

Figure 6-52

Figure 6-53

232　*Try unusual materials*

Figure 6-54

Figure 6-55

Sometimes two people operating one puppet is more effective. A stage area requiring very little construction can be set up. If students can stand on chairs or a table, they can operate their marionettes on the floor from above. Alternately, they can stand on the floor and operate the marionettes over a cardboard or cloth that covers most of their bodies. In either case, curtains can be arranged to cover the puppeteers so that only strings will show. A quick set-up is a table turned on its side. The surface can be decorated with scenery and props and students can hide behind it. The marionettes can be hung on the table legs when not performing.

The hands and knees are moved by pulling up the strings where they come through the holes in the stick. With a little practice, the marionettes can wave, cover their eyes, walk up steps or sit down. Walking is done easily by tilting the foot stick back and forth while moving the marionette forward. The action of the puppet can be simplified because of the complication of the marionette's construction and appearance. Also, fluidity of movement will be achieved with this type of puppet, so small movements will be more obvious.

Variation:

The marionettes can be made in pairs, such as an athlete and a coach, Dracula and a victim, a bride and groom, twins, or Hansel and Gretel. Mention this to your students so that they can collaborate if they so desire.

Uses:

The main purpose of this lesson is responsibility development. After basic directions are given at each phase, students should follow through on their own time, if necessary. Taking care of the project and developing a relationship with the character will help the students' own development.

Obviously, these marionettes can be made to represent a certain period in history, or designed to depict a character in some particular area of study. Then skits and programs can be written involving the puppets.

7

New dimensions in painting

Give students brushes, paint and an area to cover, and they will be completely contented! This chapter, however, offers different methods and new twists to familiar painting procedures. You will find sponges, brayers, and cotton swabs being used instead of brushes, and the paintings ranging from petite to body-size on a variety of backgrounds.

hey, that's me!
(body tracing)

Grade Levels: K-1   **Time Needed: 80 minutes**

Before You Begin:

The fun of tracing around a friend's body and then trading places is exciting in itself. Also, youngsters love to paint and rarely get an opportunity to paint on a large area. Tell your students that they will trace around each other on the large paper and then make a life-sized painting of themselves. Watch their faces light up!

Objectives:

- To present an opportunity to draw and paint larger than usual.
- To reinforce the concept of self and recognizing details relating to self-image.
- To develop drawing and painting skills with the use of crayons and brush.
- To create a unique finished product.

Materials:

- 24" x 36" white vellum drawing paper
- 18" x 24" white vellum drawing paper
- crayons
- tape
- poster paints (assorted colors including flesh tones)
- large and small brushes
- small juice cans
- mirror

Procedure:

1. Choose a partner in order to draw around each other.
2. Have the partner lie down on the large paper and get comfortable. Check to see that every part of the body is on the paper. If more paper is

needed, tape the additional paper to the original sheet. Turn shoes to the side when they need to be traced; they are easier to recognize this way.

3. Using any colored crayon, trace the partner completely. Tell students to look straight down at their partner and draw around the outside rather than under the legs and arms. Any little mistakes can be covered with paint later. Trade places and trace partners.

4. Prepare the paints. If you do not have flesh-colored paint, it can be made easily by adding a little each of red, yellow, and brown to a good amount of white. All the colors that will be needed for details cannot be provided in paint, so tell students to paint only the main colors. Remind them that anything white does not have to be painted, just outlined.

5. Pour the necessary colors of paint into the juice cans, one can for each color.

6. Take care not to paint right next to a wet area or the two colors will "bleed" together. Remember that one basic color on an area can be done first as for stripes or plaids. After it dries, add other paints or possibly crayons on top, if the area has been painted with a light-colored paint.

7. Add face details, buttons, colors, belts, glasses, shoelaces, etc., in crayon. Students should look in a mirror to check on details they can't see. Keep in mind that the painting is to be a self-portrait, so use colors and details that are the most realistic to what is seen. (See Figure 7-1.)

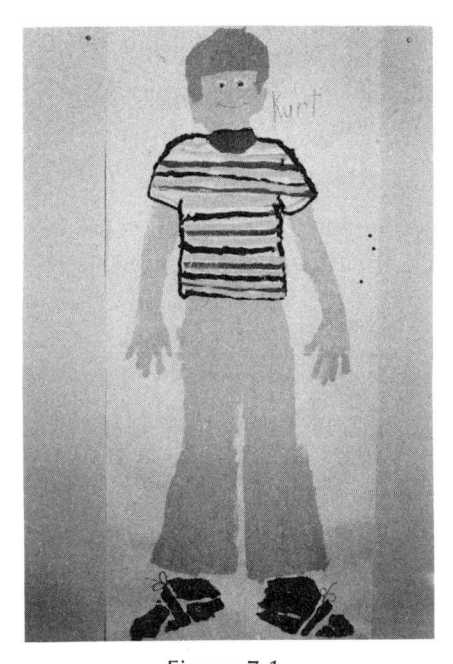

Figure 7-1

Variations:

Students can use the same technique of tracing and painting for the face, hands, and hair, but add different clothing. They might paint the person they would like to emulate: Dad, Mom, an historic figure, or a sports hero. Other themes might be:

> What I'll be when I grow up.
> How I'll dress for Halloween.
> Me as Santa Claus .. the Easter Bunny ... an Elf.

Uses:

The self-portraits make a terrific display—paint drips, footprints, and all. Place them around the classroom or in the hallway.

They could also be cut out and taped to the students' chairs, in which case students will find their "doubles" will already be sitting in their chairs.

New dimensions in painting

big green dragon
(brayer painting)

Grade Levels: K-3 **Time Needed: 80 minutes**

Before You Begin:

Read a dragon story to your students and show them pictures of dragons. This will give them some ideas of long necks, long tails, fat bodies, crested backs and tails, wings, fiery mouths, etc. Then tell the students that they are going to paint a green dragon THIS BIG (show the size of the paper)—without using a brush. This will certainly interest them! Demonstrate and display a few dragons going in both directions—or all the dragons will be heading west!

Objectives:

- To develop gross and fine motor control.
- To introduce a new tool (brayer) for painting.
- To encourage thinking and performing on a large scale.
- To stimulate creative thinking.
- To create an unusual and individual product.

Materials:

- 24" x 36" white vellum drawing paper or 36" or more of brown kraft paper
- brayers
- green poster paint (assorted shades). (NOTE: Add blue, brown or yellow to make sea green, army green, or pea green.)
- household sponges
- glue
- crayons
- scissors
- ribbon, rickrack, felt scraps, buttons, sequins
- plastic moving eyes (optional)
- smocks

Procedure:

1. Put a variety of green paint-filled sponges out but tell students to use one shade only for their dragon. Otherwise, all sponges will become the same shade!

2. Roll the brayer on a paint-filled sponge. Then roll it on the paper in the shape desired. Use the brayer to form skinny parts by rolling short strokes in rows. For fat parts, use the brayer with abandon. The points along the back and tail can easily be rolled in at angles, letting only one end of the brayer emerge from the solid body.

3. Allow enough time for the painting to dry before adding details. Glue on ribbon, trim, sequins, and buttons for emphasizing such details as scales, fire from nostrils or mouths, teeth, and horns. Use crayons to add ground, water, people, fire, and claws. One or two plastic moving eyes might be glued on a base of felt, but felt and buttons could be used instead. (See Figure 7-2.) Students can name their dragons or dictate short stories to be stapled to the painting.

Figure 7-2

Variations:

The brayer can be used to paint large "bodies" of people—Santa Claus in red, or Frosty the Snowman in white. The brayers can be used for other large animals, too, like elephants, dinosaurs, and giraffes.

The brayer also lends itself to painting designs where several colors are used, one brayer after another, to create compositions and arrangements of colors.

Mixing colors can occur at elementary level if only primary paint colors are made available to make the secondaries. Show the students that using yellow and blue (primaries) together will eventually make green (a secondary). By the same token, red and yellow will make orange and blue and red will make purple. Be prepared with a bucket of water to rinse the brayers so that all students can try the mixing process themselves. Only a little paint is needed if sponges are used to contain the paint.

Uses:

Now that you have a bunch of dragons, try making a display of them in a hallway. Th students might also display them in the cafeteria or lunch room with such captions as "Our feet aren't 'dragon.' We're very busy in class!" or "How about 'dragon' a friend to the library?"

new dimensions in painting 241

stone age cave paintings
(chalk drawings)

Grade Levels: 4-6   Time Needed: 80 minutes

Before You Begin:

Tell your students the story of the most important discovery of cave drawings. It will ceraintly interest them! The cave, in Lascaux, France, was discovered in 1940 by a group of school boys searching for their lost dog. One of these boys, Jacques Marsal, grew up to become a technician who made regular visits to the cave to check on its condition. Jacques became its official guide when the cave was opened to the public in 1948. *(The New York Times,* January 4, 1970.) This story is found in almost any encyclopedia or basic book on cave art. Show any prints or pictures you have, including the sketches pictured in this lesson, and talk about cavemen and the animals they hunted. You might want to show your students the film "Lascaux—Cradle of Man's Art." The film is available through any large library that handles educational visual aids.

Objectives:

- To learn about the discovery of the beginnings of recorded art.
- To provide an opportunity to create individually for a total plan.
- To experience a new media and technique.

Materials:

- 12" x 18" or 18" x 24" brown, tan, or gray construction paper
- shallow water containers
- colored chalks
- prints, pictures and basic sketches of cave drawings (see Figure 7-3)

Procedure:

1. Take the sheet of paper and crinkle it up a few times. Then smooth it out flat. This will give the appearance of a rough wall and will make the paper more pliable for the final display.

242   *New dimensions in painting*

Figure 7-3

2. Choose a few bright colors from the chalk assortment, along with red, yellow, black, and earth tones. Dunk the chalk in water a few times while drawing and coloring in the animal figures. (See Figure 7-4.) Use black and white for shading and highlights. The chalk will apply more smoothly and be more representative of the way the paintings were done originally. Add details such as arrows, hunters, and sun or moon, to tell a "hunting story."

Variation:

You may want to put up paper prior to drawing to have an ongoing place for students to work while studying the Stone Age. The paper, even brown kraft paper, should still be crinkled. Take the whole measured piece and wrinkle it before stapling or taping it to the bulletin board or wall. You will not be able to have lumps and bumps in this case, as drawing will be difficult if the surface is not flat.

Uses:

Show these drawings in a variety of dramatic ways. The simplest is to mount each painting on a larger backing paper or cardboard with staples or tape.

new dimensions in painting 243

Figure 7-4

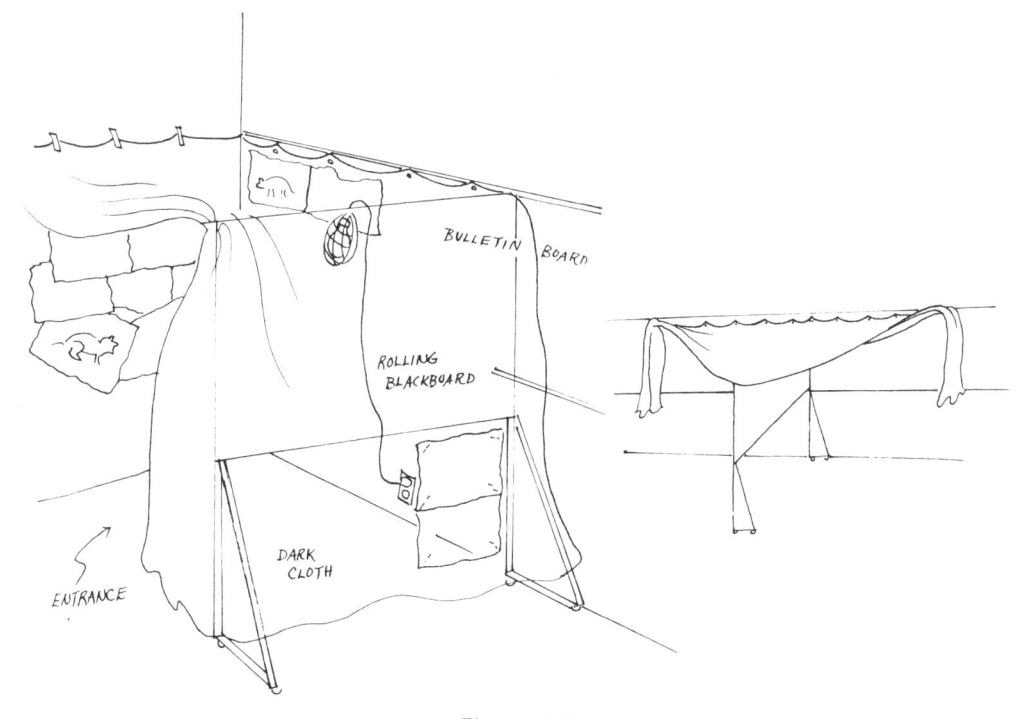

Figure 7-5

A more effective display is made on a bulletin board by first covering it with one of the original paper colors used, or even brown paper bags. Then staple on each picture by gathering corners and stapling tucks and pockets in the paper to form a rough wall-like look.

To get an authentic cave effect, use a bulletin board or wall plus a rolling blackboard or cabinet that can be placed perpendicular to the wall. Place the movable wall in the center of the base wall and use both sides. A dark cloth can be tossed over the top with a few pictures pinned to the "ceiling" and a small lamp used to light up the "cave" for viewing. (See Figure 7-5.)

bleaching everything but the laundry

(designs on material and paper)

Grade Levels: 4-6   **Time Needed: 80 minutes**

Before You Begin:

Demonstrate the use of the cotton swab, brush, and bleach on material and paper. Your students will enjoy the color-changing effect that occurs and the variety of lines and shapes that can be made. You may want to illustrate a random design or something realistic. (See Figure 7-6.) Make several finished examples prior to the lesson so that the students will know what to expect from the lesson.

Figure 7-6

Objectives:

- To develop composition within a format.
- To demonstrate a different painting technique involving unusual medium and tools.

246 New dimensions in painting

- To encourage direct work without preliminary sketching.

Materials:

- any color cotton material or "tested for bleach" blends
- dark-colored construction paper
- tape
- scissors
- heavy cardboard
- cotton swabs
- old paint brushes
- small containers
- household bleach
- smocks
- marking pens

Procedure:

1. This technique may be done on dark-colored construction paper or cloth.

2. If cloth is to be used, measure the cardboard and make the cloth piece one inch larger all around. Tape the corners of the material to the back of the cardboard by pulling it tautly over all four corners. Then tape the four sides to make a "canvas" to work on.

3. Before starting the painting, keep in mind the effects of bleach on clothing or in the eyes.

4. The bleach will "bleed" when applied to the surface so remember that applying dabs of bleach close together will result in a totally bleached-out area. The swabs are used for dots and the brushes for filling in areas. NOTE: If separate details are needed, use the brush or swab lightly, quickly, and with plenty of space between strokes.

5. Designs or pictures will be done directly in bleach without a preliminary sketch so students may want to experiment on scrap cloth or paper before beginning. Suggest a theme ... trees work very well for this technique. Snowflakes or falling leaves can be added to a brush-drawn tree. Animals, spotted and striped, space scenes, fireworks and flowers are also effective.

6. After the bleached areas are *thoroughly* dry, use marking pens to bring out details but not to fill in bleached areas. Use fine lines in patterns to decorate in and around the bleach design. (See Figures 7-7 and 7-8.)

new dimensions in painting 247

Figure 7-7

Figure 7-8

Variation:

Bleaching may be done on dark-colored T-shirts. Set the finished designs by rinsing thoroughly to get rid of excess bleach. Markers should not be used unless they are of the permanent type. Maybe your students could paint trees on their shirts to make "tree-shirts"!

Uses:

The material designs can be made into pillows by backing them with contrasting or similar material, sewing them together, then stuffing.

The finished paper designs might be displayed as they are, or mounted on contrasting paper backgrounds. The cardboard canvases need only a bit of string or yarn taped on the back by which they can be hung as paintings.

blow-up cartoons
(graphing from small to large)

Grade Levels: 5-6   **Time Needed: eight to ten 40-minute periods**

Before You Begin:

Cartoons are fun for children of all ages, who enjoy copying from comic strips, greeting cards, or advertisements. Collect cartoons for a file that can be used for this lesson, but keep in mind some restrictions: there should be no well-known characters such as Snoopy or Mickey Mouse. Animals and people are fine because these can be elaborated upon or changed by students.

Make up a small and a large sketch to give your students an idea of what they are expected to do.

Objectives:

- To introduce a new drawing method.
- To develop awareness in spatial relationships.
- To increase drawing skills.
- To provide an opportunity for color selection and combinations.
- To create a lasting final product.
- To develop original thinking and performance.

Materials:

- 8" x 12" drawing paper
- pencils
- erasers
- rulers
- colored pencils
- 24" x 36" white vellum drawing paper
- yardsticks or long straightedges
- black marking pens (thick-tipped, permanent)
- newspaper to cover work area
- poster paints (assorted colors)
- coffee cans with lids

- juice concentrate cans
- brushes
- cartoon file
- transparent plastic notebook sleeves (optional)

Procedure:

1. Look through the cartoon file for some ideas for one or more original cartoon characters that will fill out the whole 8" x 12" sketch paper without concern for background. Ground lines to divide grass or water from sky can be added when the cartoon is completed.

2. Never plagiarize someone else's work; use parts of different characters and get ideas from the file for positions of bodies. Develop an original character by changing clothes, setting, etc.

3. One character can be developed into a few for the poster, but use no more than three as they will become too small and detailed. The idea here is to draw as large as possible. Possibly one monkey could become a family of monkeys in a barrel, or a kitten could be developed into a few in a basket. Two characters that go together may make a good composition—a cat and a dog, or a frog and a fish. (See Figure 7-9.) Try a human and animal combination, such as a tiger and a trainer. Inanimate objects can be used together with animals or people if they are interesting. A dog and a doghouse may be boring, but a dog dressed as a boxer in a boxing ring with part of a knocked-out opponent may be more fun to draw and paint. The tall man and little pig would not fill out the poster because of their diverse sizes, so the wagons were added to develop the characters and the theme. (See Figure 7-10.)

4. Once the sketch is completed, graph it with a colored pencil into one-inch squares to make the drawing easier to "read." Number the boxes

Figure 7-9

250   *New dimensions in painting*

across the top and down one side as a guide when enlarging begins. Slip the sketch into a plastic cover for protection.

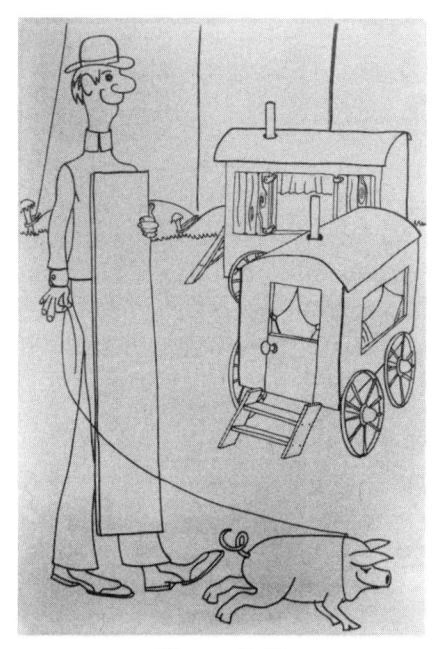

Figure 7-10

5. Now, lightly graph the 24" x 36" paper into three-inch squares. Use a regular pencil. If yardsticks are scarce, use 12-inch rulers to mark off at three-inch intervals and use long straightedges to connect the dots. Number the poster squares to correspond with the sketch so that drawing can begin.

6. Fill in each square as it is shown on the small sketch, but remember that the drawing is nine times larger. Examine each square carefully and draw exactly *what* is seen *where*. The negative areas are as important as the positive, so remember to look at the empty areas of each box and try to reproduce those as well as the actual areas that are parts of the picture. NOTE: A trick for areas with a lot of details is to "windowpane" the square on the sketch and its counterpart on the poster. (See Figure 7-11.) This helps to insure that the drawing is exact because it provides four small squares wihin the larger square, enabling students to work in a more detailed and accurate manner.

7. Occasionally view the whole artwork at once, to spot drastic errors before they become difffficult to change. Drawing should be light to facilitate erasing.

new dimensions in painting 251

Figure 7-11

    8. Upon completion of the sketch, trace the drawing with the thickest edge of the black marker to achieve a "page-in-a-coloring-book" effect. Make sure all lines bump into each other or run off the edge to form areas for each separate color. The lines should also be smooth and solid as opposed to sketchy. Fill in small black areas, such as pupils of eyes, noses on animals, or stripes and spots, with the marker. Don't forget to use newspaper under the drawings or there will be duplicates on the tables and floor!

    9. Erase extraneous pencil marks, including most of the graph lines. Then start painting.

    10. Prepare the poster paints, using coffee cans that can be closed between painting sessions. Provide small fruit juice cans to pour small amounts of paint for individual students. These can be washed out. Otherwise, paint directly from the can. Allow students to choose a few brushes in various sizes to fill in the painting. Clean them out between colors by swishing them in a can of water and drying with paper towels. This reduces the splashing of water all over the surrounding area and paintings! Newspapers are not needed under the paintings, as they make the room messy and also cause paint spillage. Instead, have small pieces of newspaper for each student to place under his or her can of paint and brushes. When painting near an edge, just slide a piece of paper along under the poster to protect table or floor. Encourage painting only one color inside each area created by the black lines. NOTE: The colors most

likely to be needed for this project are the primaries and the secondaries. (Replace purple with a lighter shade by adding some to white. The purple is almost black and also stains.) White is needed as even white areas should be painted. Brown in several shades for dogs, bears, and monkeys can be made by adding white, red, and orange to regular brown. Make plenty of sky blue and several shades of green for grass, water, reptiles, etc. Mix white, yellow, brown, and blue to regular green for light green, pea green, army green, and sea green. Pink (start with white and add a bit of red) and flesh (for human characters) will be needed. Add a little each of yellow, red, and brown to white to make flesh. Black is needed for large areas that cannot be filled in with the marker. Make gray by starting with white and adding small amounts of black. The amount of paint needed can be judged if you've painted with your classes before. Provide a one-pound can of each color with doubles of sky blue, gray, and some browns for about 150 students. For one class, a quarter of a can of each color plus more of the popular colors should be sufficient.

11. Once the painting is complete and dry, use a marker to touch up the poster, retracing marker lines where necessary. Also add any other details needed to complete the drawing, such as whiskers, buttons, etc. For protection and permanency, the painting can be laminated, framed under glass, or mounted on a wall under plexiglass.

Variation:

The posters can be made directly on large paper without the enlarging process, but the idea of graphing will teach the students a technique that they may find useful in future projects. For example, a magazine or book may have to be used for research for some academic work, and an overlay of a grid on tracing paper could be used to enlarge the picture.

Uses:

There are countless uses for this technique, including map drawings, animal research, and portraits.

The finished posters present a very colorful display, and individually make great decorations. You might want to have the students display the small sketch along with the final poster in order to show the progress from small to large.

Index

A

Accuracy, in puppet-making, 50
Animals:
    origami puppets, 49-55
    torn-paper, 25-28
Animation techniques, 69-73
Associations, bizarre, expressing through art, 78-80
Arrangements:
    asymmetrical, 101
    symmetrical, 101
    techniques, 30
Art:
    basic principles of, 101
    beginnings of, 241-244
    "button," 122
Art distortion, 74-77
Autobiographies, using puppets for, 33
Axis, 155, 163

B

Balloons, in cartoons, 121
Bas-relief crayon rubbings, 101-103
Bleaching, 245-247
Block letters, 85-89
Body tracing, 235-237
Bone structure, 37
Bookmaking, 209-214
Brayer, for painting, 238-240
"Button art," 122

C

Camping, as craft theme, 60
Carbon paper designs, 104-106
Cartoons, 29-31
    "balloons" in, 121
    basics of, 119
    blow up, 248-252
    contour drawing, 159-162
    developing spatial relationships, 248-252
    development of, 118
Cave drawing, 241-244
Chalk drawings, 241-244
Charcoal printing, 98-100
Christmas:
    decorations, 44
    paper dolls for, 82-84
    printing for, 97
Circus:
    printing a motif, 98-100
    tents, 64
Clay:
    bead jewelry, 192-195
    dagging, 193
    for history lessons, 192-195
    self-expression with, 108
    slipping, 193-194
    wedging, 109
Color:
    arrangement of, 85
    effects of overlaying, 125-127
    sense, 98
    use of, 85
Coloring skills, 98
Compass, familiarity with, 42
Composition, 104
    development of, 74, 98
    techniques, 30
Composites, for paper dolls, 81-84
Contour, 156
    drawing technique, 159-162
    for visual expression, 123
Converging lines, 129

254 Index

Coordination, small motor, 25
Costumes, for puppets, 183-185
Crafts, with unusual materials, 179-233
Crayon rubbings, 101-103
   bas-relief, 101-103
Crayons:
   painting with, 235-237
   with polyethylene sheeting, 125-127
Creative thinking, developing, 30
Creativity, 60
   drawing as outlet, 119
Cut paper decorations, 45-48
Cutting:
   accuracy in, 60
   intricate, 65

D

Dagging, 193
Designs:
   basic elements, 22
   carbon paper for, 104-106
   compass, 44
   effective, 140
   letter, 152-154
   name, 152-154
   non-objective, 107
   objective, 107
   on material, 245-247
   on paper, 245-247
   ruler, 44
   within framework, 45, 81
Dimensions, demonstrating two and three, 34-36, 186
Directions, following:
   block letters, 85
   learning to, 37
   visual, 85
Distortion, meaning of, 74-77
Dolls:
   composites for, 81-84
   Halloween, 84
   paper
      for Christmas, 82-84
      for Easter, 84
      St. Patrick's day, 84
   sewing, 205-208
   stuffed, 205-208
   three-dimensional, 205-208
   writing encouraged by, 208
Dragons, for painting, 238-240
Dramatization, using puppets for, 55
Drawing:
   chalk, 241-244

Drawing (cont'd.)
   contour, 159-162
   copy work, 98-100
   detailed, 81-84
   graphing, 248-252
   mistakes in, 94
   objects, 155-158
   six formulas for people, 148-151
   skills, 104
Drawings, cave, 241-244

E

Easter:
   decorating for, 25, 31
   paper dolls for, 84
   rabbits for, 45-48
Eggs, for cartoons, 29-31
Ellipse, 113, 156
Expression:
   comic, 30
   new elements in, 78-80
   realistic, 92
   through puppets, 50
Expressions, facial, 119-122
Eyes:
   movement of, 69-73
   shape of, 69

F

Faces:
   drawing, 167-169
   for Halloween, 72-73
   highlighting, 69-73
   shadowing, 69-73
   storybook characters, 72-73
Facial features:
   drawing, 69-73
   how to make, 52-53
Figures:
   historical, 84
   paper, 81-84
   six formulas for drawing, 148-151
Finger puppets, 186-188
Fingerprints, 91-93
"Fired," 108
Folding, 104-106
   accuracy in, 60
Foresight, in creating figures, 81
Form, three-dimensional, 32
Formulas, for drawing people, 148-151
Frontals, drawing, 163-166

Index

G

Games, to loosen up skills, 116-118
Gifts, making vs. buying, 56
Glove characters, 189-191
Graphing, 248-252

H

Haiku, 201, 203
Halloween:
   crafts for, 37-40
   decorations, 72-73
   paper dolls for, 84
   printing for, 94-97
Headgear, 215-217
Hearts:
   and flowers, 140-143
   uses for, 59
Hex signs, 143
History:
   clay bead jewelry for, 192-195
   weaving and Indian designs, 199
Holidays:
   Christmas
      decorations, 44
      paper dolls for, 82-84
      printing for, 97
   Easter
      decorating for, 25, 31
      paper dolls for, 84
      rabbits for, 45-48
   Halloween
      crafts for, 37-40
      decorations for, 72-73
      dolls for, 84
      faces for, 72-73
      printing for, 94-97
   St. Patrick's day
      dolls for, 84
   Valentine's day
      cards, 56-59
Horizon, 129
Horizontal, definition of, 129
Houses:
   drawing, 170-178
   paper models, 63-64
Humor, expressing through art, 78-80

I

Idea, "inventing," 79
Interaction, through masks, 215-217
Interpretation, realistic, 136

J

Jewelry, clay bead, 192-195

K

Kiln, 108

L

"Lascaux—Cradle of Man's Art," 241
Letters, block, 85-89
Light, use of in drawing, 42
Line drawings, elaborating on, 145-147
Listening, developing skill, 37

M

Magazines:
   for creating humor, 78
   for creating mystery, 78
   use of for art, 74-77
Marbleizing, 209-214
Marionettes, 218-233
Masks, foam, 215-217
Mitten characters, 189-191
Mobiles:
   no-mess, 34-36
   snake design, 22-24
   telephone wire, 196-200
Mural work, 151
Mystery, expressing through art, 78-80

O

Object drawing, 155-158
Origami, for puppets, 49-55
Overlaying, effects of color, 125-127
Outdoor scenes, 60-64

P

Painting:
   body tracing, 235-237
   brayer, 238-240
   new dimensions in, 234-251
   self-portraits, 235-237
Paper:
   basic skills with, 21-40
   cutting techniques, 56-59
   folding techniques, 56-59
Paper models, 60-64

Paper tearing, 25-28
  objects for, 28
Parallel, 129
Pennsylvania Dutch art, 140-143
People, six formulas for drawing, 148-151
Perforations, for drawing, 42-44
Perspective:
  definition, 128-134
  one-point, 128-134
  two-point, 170-178
Picture plane, 129
Pictures, perforated light, 42-44
Planets, study of, 44
Plants, drawing, 113-115
Plate, definition of, 101
Polyethylene sheeting, 125-127
Poetry:
  haiku, 201, 203
  rhyming, 201, 203-204
  three-dimensional, 201-204
Pop-art, 29-31
Potpourri, photo, 78-80
Press, making, 107-111
Principles, art:
  arrangement, 101
  color, 101
  composition, 101
  shapes, 101
Printing, 90-111
Profiles, drawing, 163-166
Proportion, measuring, 155-158
Puppets, *see also* "Marionettes"
Puppets, 180-182
Puppets:
  accuracy in making, 50
  clothes for, 183-185
  dramatization with, 55
  effective, 49
  finger, 186-188
  origami, 49-55
  outlets for expression, 32
  paper-mouth, 32-33
  teaching three-dimensional form, 32
  uses for, 55
Pussy willows, in printing, 91-93

R

Rabbits, as decorations, 45-48
Realism, 113
Relationships, spatial, 248-252
Responsibility, development of through marionettes, 218-233
Rubbings, crayon, 101-103

S

Scenery:
  outdoor, 60-64
  three-dimensional, 65-68
Scissors, cartoon making with, 123-124
Sculpture:
  and creative writing, 201-204
  natural materials for, 201-204
  paper, 34-36
  soft, 215-217
  techniques, 34-36
Self-image, using puppets for, 33
Self-portraits, 235-237
Setup, 155
Sewing, dolls, 205-208
Sheeting, polyethylene, 125-127
Skeletons, 37-40
Skills:
  coloring, 98, 104
  cutting, 45
  drawing, 98, 104
  manipulative, 78, 108
  observation, 78
Slipping, 193-194
Snakes, introduction to drawing, 22-23
Snowmen, 42-44
Spirals, how to draw, 22-23
Spring, decorations for, 45-48
St. Patrick's Day, paper dolls for, 84
Stampers, 107-111
Stars, study of, 44
"Stations," use of in block letters, 85
"Station point," 171
Supplies, total use of, 45
Symmetry, 92, 94-97, 98-100, 104, 140, 155

T

Techniques:
  animation, 69-73
  connective, 34-36
  construction, basic, 60-64
  contour, 159-162
  drawing, 104
  letter-making, 85
  lettering, 152-154
  painting, 92
  puppet-making, 49-55
  sculpture, 34-36
Tents, for crafts themes, 60
The Natural Way to Draw, 159, 160
Three-dimensional:
  dolls, 205-208

Three-dimensional *(cont'd.)*
   pictures, 128-134
   poetry, 201-204
   scenery, 65-68
Tools, using common objects for, 108
Tracing, body, 235-237
Trees, drawing, 135-139

U

"U's" and "V's", in drawing, 135-139

V

Valentine cards, 56-59
   elaborate, 56-59
   uses for, 59
Value, definition of, 167-169
Vanishing point, 128-129, 171
Vellum:
   for printing, 94

Vellum *(cont'd.)*
   use of, 45
Vertical, definition of, 129
Vignette, meaning of, 69-73

W

Wallpaper, use of for puppets, 54
Warp, 196-200
Weaving:
   spider-web, 196
   telephone wire mobiles, 196-200
Wedging, 109
Weft, 196-200
Writing:
   dolls for, 208
   encouraging, 31, 77
   printing as basis for, 93
   sculpture and, 201-204
   using photo potpourri for, 80
   using puppets for, 55